21 CRYPTO SECRETS

That turned 4 figures into 6 figures in less than 12 months

Hey Therese!
Hope this book brings you
all the success!

Devin Milsom

Contents

Foreword

The only thing that's guaranteed in life is change; changing economies, changing cultures, and changing technology. We live in an unprecedented time, where the rate of change has never been more obvious and pervasive. Go back 100 years and a person may have seen one or two major changes in their life time, but nothing more drastic than that – fast forward to 2018, and our generation is experiencing technological paradigm shifts almost on a monthly basis. Self-driving electric cars, space travel, super computers that fit in your palm and in your pocket, but probably the most exciting of them all is… Blockchain Technology.

In terms of technology that has the potential to completely change the face of the Earth, Blockchain is a major player in the space of disrupting industries worldwide. The distributed decentralised ledger technology using the science of cryptography that's been evolving since the conception of Bitcoin in 2008 – the first digital decentralised asset to become a real store of value – is set to both revolutionise and completely destroy multiple industries from voting systems to insurance contracts, and of course, currency.

How we store and exchange value has been changing over the last 10 years, and we sit now on the cusp of mass adoption of this still relatively new technology. No longer will centralised financial institutions command power and control over the masses, no longer will global conglomerates hoard power in secrecy, and no longer will governments be able to get away with distorting and withholding information from their people. Everything is about to change, and this brings with it a tenuous mix of excitement for the possibility of what may become possible, and a dawning realisation that such drastic change will not be without its challenges and growing pains.

There will be resistance, there will be opposition, and there will be naysayers. So how can one be expected to sort the truth from the lies, and set oneself up to ride the wave of change that is all but inevitable? In any emerging market, new technology or new ideas there are always the few brave early adopters who make the continued evolution of those things possible – without them, new ideas, technologies and markets would fail to get the traction they need to really have a chance at propagating in the world. These people are the catalyst of evolution and innovation, and we need them now more than ever.

That's why I'm so excited about this space, and about this book – '21 Crypto Secrets' is a deep diving into this brave new technology that will not only give you the knowledge you need to understand all things Crypto, but will also set you up with the skills you need to position yourself so you can profit from what is set to be the biggest boom in technology since the DotCom 'bubble'. Never mind the exciting technological prospects for Blockchain technology, the potential to profit from this new emerging market as these assets become adopted and used by the masses worldwide is unprecedented. The question is, are you going to be riding the wave? Or are you going to get dumped into the water head first and swept out to sea?

I started trading Bitcoin back in 2016 when it was a mere $800 per coin – who wouldn't want to get their hands on an $800 Bitcoin today? Here's the thing though, I had no idea what I was doing, and although I'd be researching the space for the last 3 years, finding high quality information amongst all the disinformation was a full-time job in itself. The truth is, I knew that this was going to be big, I knew that this technology was going to change the world, but understanding how to be a part of that was somewhat more complex. If only this book had existed when I came to the markets in 2016 – my results would have been a lot different... and with a lot more upside! Since then I have taught myself the art of trading and investing in Crypto Assets, and now have a healthy 5-figure portfolio that's perfectly positioned for the next bull run, and set to explode into 6 or even 7 figures over the next few years, without doing much at all. Having read the 21 secrets here in this book, and working with Devin closely for several months now, I know that with just a small amount of effort I can produce massive amounts of personal wealth using some very simply strategies shared in the later chapters of this book.

Why am I telling you this? Well, because I desperately want the same for you and your family. I believe money is a powerful tool that creates limitless options in the lives of those who control it – and there's more than enough to go around! I believe everyone not only has a right but an obligation to be wealthy. With wealth comes great responsibility, and those with money have the power to effect massive positive change in the world. During my time coaching business owners, I've had the privilege of meeting several multi-millionaires and I can tell you that they have all blown me away with their desire to contribute and to help make the world a better place. They donate generously to great causes all over the world, saving lives, educating millions and giving people the tools they need to fight their way to a better life, and a better world. This is the gift Devin and I want to give to you – the power to make both your life and the world around you the best it can possibly be.

With money comes choices, and choices are what life is all about. How badly do you want to spend your time doing the things you love, with the people you love, on your terms? Yeah, me too.

When I met Devin, I knew instantly that he was someone I needed to be working with as he values empowering people and changing the world as much as I do. That's why he studies the Blockchain and Crypto Asset space diligently and obsessively on a daily basis – so he can disseminate the best information about the space back out to all of you. When it comes to experts, Devin is my go-to guy in the world of Crypto and Blockchain, and I'm thrilled that he's sharing his best insights and what he's learned over his years of study with you here in this book. Devin and I have been working tirelessly to bring this information out to you for many months now, and to create a business that would serve the growing community of crypto-enthusiasts, supporters and evangelists so that you too can be a part of something that is changing the world as we know it on a daily basis.

Welcome to The Club; with the knowledge in this book, you're no longer one of those people merely dipping their toe in the waters of change – you're swimming in it, and I'm excited to see what you'll do for yourself and for the world with the information you're about to learn.

Let's ride the wave together; let us be the drivers, the misfits and the early adopters who together will change the world for the better.

Jamie Keeling

Elite Business Coach & Crypto Investor

Introduction

The cryptocurrency market is not an easy market to be in. It is wildly volatile and unforgiving to newer investors. I've learnt lessons the hard way, and lost a lot of money doing so. After hundreds of hours committed to learning everything I can about cryptocurrencies, investing and trading, I finally learnt how to overcome the traps that I see many newer investors falling for and that I fell for myself. My main inspiration for writing this book is to help you avoid these traps and provide you with the knowledge to make a substantial return on your investment in this emerging asset class. There are countless "experts" in this market, and I have followed many before, only to be stung by their ill-founded advice and then later finding out that they have hidden agendas. I've fallen for scams, I've invested in dodgy ICOs, I've lost money on exchanges, I've fallen for pump and dump groups and I've also believed those "experts" that know which coin is going to boom next... they don't. These lessons were costly for me, but I am glad they happened. Because without them I would have never turned £5,500 into over £175,000 in less than 12 months and been able to become a full-time investor/trader. I've paid the price so you don't have to, and I firmly believe that you need to take your investments into your own hands. I hope this book can be the foundation for you confidently investing in the cryptocurrency market, knowing what is likely a scam and what is a solid investment.

Before we dive into the 21 secrets that helped me grow my portfolio by over 3,000%, I want to share my story with you…

Flash back to early 2015. I had just finished my final year of college and all of my friends were celebrating their offers from various universities. I remember awkwardly replying to everyone who asked which universities I got into with "I didn't apply," and you should have seen the look on their faces. Without them saying anything, I could hear them thinking, "What are you doing with your life?" I knew that going to university wasn't the path for me and it was the most difficult decision of my life (I didn't have many decisions to make up until that point lol). I felt judged by my teachers, my friends and even my family. I didn't want to let them down, but I knew I'd be letting myself down by following the 'traditional' route. It just didn't make sense to me; the average degree would have put me in debt for around £50K and after reading *Rich Dad, Poor Dad*, I knew that I needed to focus on assets, not liabilities.

I've always had an entrepreneurial mindset and have always been fascinated with investing. It's been my passion from a young age. I idolized famous investors like Warren Buffet and Robert Kiyosaki and aspire to one day achieve the level of success that they have had. But back in 2015, I had hardly any money – £0 compounded will always be £0. I knew I had to get a job, at least for the short term, until I could generate enough cash flow to invest/start my own business.

I landed a job with an insurance broker as a trainee, the typical "safe" corporate 9-5 job. Being a trainee, I was left with just £1,000 per month after taxes to spend. Luckily, I didn't have any major expenses at the time so I was putting around £500 per month into investments and attempting to start my own businesses. After a few failed businesses and thousands of pounds lost attempting to day trade, I almost gave up and accepted the reality of following the path of many who have lived before me. Graduate from college, get a job, climb the ladder, get married, have 2.4 children, retire and die. I wanted to create my own ladder, take control of my own life. But reality hit me: it is not as easy as it looked in *The Wolf of Wall Street.* I spent the next few months working harder than anyone in the office, even those who were 20 years older than me. I got in early, and I stayed late. I did anything and everything I could to be the best. I passed all my qualifications before anyone else. I honestly felt good – I thought, *At this rate I'll be doubling or tripling my income in no time.* How naive! I remember having a sit down with my boss to discuss promotions and being told that no matter what I was doing, or how well I was doing, the most I'd be on in three years was £22K, which was around £500 more per month than I was earning. The thing is, to me this felt like a complete waste of my life. I knew this wasn't the person I wanted to be. You know that feeling when you know something doesn't feel right, but you're not quite sure what? Well, that was me. Sat there in my cubicle at my insurance job, I felt empty. *This can't be it… can it?*

It was at this point in my life where I had doubts: *were my teachers, friends and family right? Am I not cut out for this entrepreneurial route?* I almost gave up but I knew deep down that I would rather fail trying than play it safe and not try at all.

I'd get home most days around 6, and then spend from 7-12 studying investors, asset classes and trends.

I really enjoyed it, and started to learn some very valuable lessons. My first introduction to cryptocurrencies was off the back of a commodities forum. They were discussing gold and the future of it and there were a few mentions of this "digital gold" called "Bitcoin". I was highly sceptical at first, but decided to do some research. This defined the turning point in my life, and after I had a reasonable understanding of blockchain, it ignited a passion for learning that some would deem unhealthy. Every evening, I would consume everything I could about Bitcoin and how it worked. It was (and still is) truly fascinating. After a few months of research, I realized that the technology behind Bitcoin would disrupt every middleman-type business out there, and being an insurance broker, I realized that I was currently one of those middlemen. I tried explaining this technology to my work colleagues but many of them didn't care and probably thought there was something wrong with me. It was kind of like the scene off of Chicken Little when he runs around screaming, "The sky Is falling", but with me saying something like "Blockchain is coming"…

It was towards the beginning of 2017 when I announced that I was going to be investing in Bitcoin and that's when I was met with the advice from everyone around me to avoid "risky" assets. Especially a "make-believe token". Again, my family, colleagues and friends were all very sceptical of me investing in this thing called Bitcoin and I don't blame them, as they didn't know anything about it. I knew that I had a much greater understanding of both the technology behind Bitcoin and how financial markets work so I decided to go against the herd for the second time in my life, and invested enough to get me 1 BTC at the time (I made the beginner's error of thinking you need to buy an entire bitcoin).

I was pretty happy at first, mainly because other than commodities (which is a long-term play) this was my first proper medium-term investment. Guess what happened in the following month after I bought it? It fell for three weeks straight, I lost 30% of my investment and I could see the look on everyone's face, saying, "I told you so". I started to lose faith. Maybe I was wrong? Maybe it was all a scam, a pyramid scheme? That's what all the media and everyone around me was saying.

The lack of certainty really motivated me to dive further into understanding both blockchain and how financial markets operate and the more I found out, the more I knew I needed to learn. It was late on a Friday night, and instead of going out clubbing, I found myself on a Bitcoin forum discussing the future of the crypto space and that is when I discovered a term that you are probably very familiar with now… Altcoin.

I had absolutely no clue what an "Altcoin" was at the time, but the best explanation was simply an alternative to Bitcoin. This really spiked curiosity for me, partially because I was currently down 30% with Bitcoin and partially because I had learnt the lessons of diversification from my finance idols.

The first Altcoin I invested in was Ethereum, it blew me away with the potential growth of the platform. Bitcoin is really just a currency, or a store of value (however you look at it). However, Ethereum is a tool that provided a solution to a decentralized future. I put most of my funds into Ethereum but this time, I didn't tell anyone – it wasn't worth the hassle.

A few months later, my initial investment in Ethereum was up near 1,000% and my Bitcoin investment was up around 300%. Both are tremendous returns, but I learnt a very valuable lesson by diversifying early on (I'll share that later).

I kept on averaging in capital to the market. By averaging in, I mean I was putting as much capital as I could into the market. I sacrificed nights out, sacrificed getting the latest clothes and games and all the other useless things we are pressured to buy and by November 2017, I had invested a total amount of £5,500 into the market. Which isn't a lot of money, but to me at the time, this was a huge investment.

Over the course of 2017, I managed to turn this small amount of £5,500 into over £175,000. I remember in January when my portfolio crossed the six-figure level I was ecstatic. Then just a few weeks later, I grew it by an additional £75,000. I remember my best week was when my portfolio increased by $ 100,000. Yes, in just a week. Now, I'm not saying this to brag. I know it may come across this way. I was proud of my achievements, mostly because I had lost a lot of money in the process of learning how to rapidly scale my portfolio like this, and it was nice to see my hard work pay off. This was not easy, and was certainly directly correlated with the market trend. By no means am I saying if you apply these secrets that you can achieve the same, but they are what got me to that level and with the right market conditions and knowledge of these secrets, who knows how high your portfolio can go. I share this also to inspire those who have entered the market during this downwards trend. I know how I felt when I was down 30% – it really sucked and I felt like I'd never see the green again. Patience is key.

In January, I made the third biggest decision of my life, and that was to quit my corporate 9-5 job. This was a massive turning point in my life, and it really wasn't an easy decision. My company didn't want to let me go, and they even spoke about a potential imminent pay rise. My parents, having worked corporate jobs their entire life, were very cautious about me quitting my "safe" job. However, they did not object, and I really thank them for this. They have always let me chase my dreams despite how risky they are. Without their support, I would struggle to be in the position I am today.

I ignored many people, as I knew their "advice" reflected their beliefs and reality. "It's too risky", "Most businesses fail" and "We'll keep your seat warm for when you're back" were comments that really annoyed me. These comments actually motivated me more to succeed in both my investments and in business. I was not made for the 9-5 corporate life, and don't get me wrong, I am not saying there is anything wrong with working 9-5 if you are happy with it. I was not happy there; I knew my potential was greater pursuing my own path.

Me leaving my job was coincidental to my portfolio being at an all-time high. I had planned to leave regardless of how high it was. Throughout 2017, I had actively been blogging and posting my articles on websites like Quora and Medium and had gathered a fairly large following from doing so. I helped hundreds of people during this time and had people offer to give me thousands as a thank you and I also remember receiving an offer of near $10,000 USD to promote a dodgy ICO to my followers. This was one of many but it was the largest single offer I received. I declined the offersbecause I valued my reputation over quick money. I really enjoy teaching and helping others grow their portfolio, I have received some emails from people who have changed their lives from their investment returns, which is great and heartwarming.

I decided in November that I would teach investors everything I knew about investing/trading cryptocurrencies and I released a course in January 2018. This helped me quit my job and focus 100% on investing/trading the cryptocurrency market. It's funny, I look back at my knowledge in January and cringe at how little I knew compared to today and even today I find that the more I learn, the more I know I need to learn. In such a rapidly evolving market, you have to be constantly learning and doing research. This is why I believe that no-one is a true expert in this field. It is an emerging market, and no-one can predict the future. There's no such thing as an expert, as to be one you'd have to know cryptography, and know to a high degree about financial markets – in particular, emerging asset classes (which doesn't happen very often). Oh, and also be able to predict the future. Please let me know if you find this person!

Now, nine months down the line, I have grown Emerging Markets Investment Club (the name of the business) into an amazing community of like-minded investors who share their knowledge and communicate on a regular basis. The best feeling is making a trading call and seeing hundreds of people profit from it (we'll be talking about this in greater detail later). I pride myself on honesty and transparency. I have been wrong and I'll more than likely be wrong again going forward. No-one is perfect. Losing is part of investing, and for those that are wondering, my portfolio is down since the January crash – however, I am still up near 2,000% and have doubled my token holdings this year, which I am proud of. I have been correct far more than wrong, and as long as my winners are far greater than my losers, I am happy, and I know the members of the club are happy too.

Then we get to where I am today; I am constantly expanding my knowledge around investing, cryptos and business. My main goal is to provide extremely valuable content and tools to help you succeed in your investing journey, and that is one of the main reasons why I wrote this book. This book is packed with actionable content, and even if you disagree with some of my points, at least it offers a different viewpoint. Confirmation bias has hurt me in the past massively. Don't make that same mistake.

To finish my story, I want to share with you my goals for the future, both for EMIC and personally.

I'll start with personally. The common joke you see in this market is that everyone is waiting for the "moon" so they can get their Lambos. I'm really not that interested in getting a fancy car or any toys until I have enough assets that can purchase those luxuries through residual income. My biggest goal is to pay off my parents' mortgage – they have helped me more than I could ever expect them to and I want to give back to them in one way or another. I also want to help as many people as possible to become financially free and have the option, if they wish to, to leave their job and do what makes them happy. It's a big goal, but it is what I am passionate about.

The goal for Emerging Market Investment Club is to become the go-to place for information about emerging markets. Cryptocurrency is the main focus for now, but markets are cyclical and there are tons of new technologies in the horizon. Where there is dramatic innovation, profits can be made. As the club grows, we will be developing more tools, expanding into other asset classes and helping as many people as possible to build enough wealth to have the option to leave their job. This vision is shared by me personally and by EMIC.

Before we move onto the next section, I want to ask you what your goals are. Many people answer, "I want to make money," but often it is more than that. Why do you want to make money? Having set goals will make your investment journey far more meaningful. Feel free to share your goals with me at: devin@emergingmarket-sinvestmentclub.com

Investing is a journey, a marathon, not a sprint. That's not to say wealth can't be accumulated in a short period – I am proof that it can. It is just to say that it might take a longer period than it took me – it might take years. Don't give up. Not just in the crypto market – there are opportunities everywhere.

I wish you all the success, and please share your achievements with me via the email address above.

Devin Milsom

What This Book Is Not

I want to begin by clarifying a few things…

This book is NOT a get rich quick scheme; there is no such thing. Cryptocurrencies are a vehicle where you can accumulate wealth rapidly, due to the infancy and volatility of the market, but there are no guarantees. Please do not invest more than you are willing to lose. The worst emails I have to read are those who have taken out loans to go into crypto and are now in debt. I started with just £5,500 and invested this amount over the course of 9 months. I was entirely able to lose this amount. Sure, no-one wants to lose money, but it wouldn't have affected me if I did.

There are no guarantees. The secrets I share have worked in the past, and I do expect many of them to continue to work going forward. I've tried to keep this book "evergreen" but the market will change over time and so will the strategies. None of these strategies are advice, merely an indication of what has worked for me in the past and what could possibly work going forward. Always do your own research and know that ultimately, you are responsible for the success or failure of your investments. When I am wrong, I don't go and blame others for it, I learn from it, and that alone has been the key to my success.

I'm not an expert, as I mentioned earlier. I will never claim to know exactly which coin will "moon" next. Yes,

I have chosen over 13 coins which have increased by more than 1,000% through the secrets that I will be sharing with you. But there are absolutely no guarantees. Investing is all about probabilities and risk allocation. One of the reasons why I created EMIC was due to certain self-proclaimed "experts" scamming people into buying their secret insider knowledge. I've read lots of emails to me where people had put their life savings into these recommended coins just for them to lose 90% of their value. This is nothing more than sleazy marketing luring those after get rich quick cryptos. So please, be careful who you trust. There is tremendous value in following people who know what they are talking about, in an honest and transparent fashion. Even though I know a great deal more than the average investor, I still follow and learn from many people (I'll share some links at the end of the book).

The End of Easy Money

Before I invested in cryptos, I spent years studying the global economy and various asset classes. It fascinates me. I could write a book about what I've learnt (and I probably will at some point). This section isn't going to be covering in depth why I believe a financial crisis is around the corner, rather how cryptos could potentially perform during this time.

We are heading into what I like to call "the end of easy money". Interest rates have sat at 0.25% from 2009 – 2016, for seven years straight, making it very easy for any person or company to take out a very inexpensive loan. Easy money. Low interest rates have killed savers, with "official" inflation hovering around the 3% level. Savers are losing 2.75% per year by sitting on their capital. With capital on tap, we have seen various asset classes skyrocket to all-time highs. The combination of very low interest rates and multiple rounds of quantitative easing have artificially boosted both the stock markets and real estate markets globally for the past 10 years.

The music is coming to an end.

Interest rates (the cost of borrowing money) are rising, and will continue to do so. See, interest rates can go up or down, we all know that. What many people do not realise is that interest rates either go up, up, up, up, up – until a recession – or down, down, down, down until the economy picks up again.

In 2004, interest rates sat at 1%. In 2008 they hit 5.25%, increasing 17 times in four years. We all know what followed after 2008.

In 2016 interest rates sat at 0.25%. Today (October 2018) interest rates are sitting at 2.25%. An 8 times increase.

I've predicted multiple interest rate increases this year, and expect at least one further hike before 2019. Then in 2019 we will see three or four further hikes. It is inevitable. I do see a financial crisis before the end of 2020. However, I am fully aware that markets tend to trend far longer and far higher than anyone can ever anticipate.

We are living in a very interesting time in history, and I'm both very excited and nervous about the future. Stock markets globally are reaching all-time highs, with price-to-earnings ratios the highest they've ever been. Property prices are continuing to soar into record-breaking territory. We are told by our governments that the economy is doing great, and shows no signs of slowing down.

This is a lie.

"The Federal Reserve is not currently forecasting a recession." – Ben Bernanke, Federal Reserve Chairman, January 10, 2008.

Asset classes are cyclical. They do not rise forever and they do not fall forever. The stock market will come crashing down, and so will the real estate market. By the time you are reading this book, it may already have happened. However, there are assets that are negatively correlated to stocks and real estate that you should be aware of.

Precious metals are seen as a safe haven during times of fear. During the financial crisis of 2008, the price of silver rose from $10 to $50 and gold rose from $700 to just under $2000. Precious metals share very similar qualities to cryptocurrencies. Unlike the dollar, both precious metals and crypto assets have fixed supplies are deflationary by nature. Just like there is only so much gold and silver that is mineable, there are only 21 million bitcoins that are minable, and over 17 million have already been mined.

So, how will cryptocurrencies perform during a financial crisis? A great question. Many crypto enthusiasts assume that cryptos will be the go-to asset class during a financial crisis. While I tend to agree (confirmation bias), I am aware that no-one truly knows. This asset class has not been battle-tested… yet. Here are the main arguments for and against crypto assets performing well during a financial crisis.

For Crypto Assets

Bitcoin is widely referred to as "digital gold". As mentioned before, during times of fear, investors are looking to preserve as much of their capital as possible, and have historically used precious metals to become a store of value. Many investors are already using Bitcoin as a store of value, despite its volatility. If everyone believes that Bitcoin is a safe haven and a store of value, then during a crisis, it may very well live up to these expectations. This is one of the most common reasons that people give.

Another reason closely tied to the first is the fear of hyperinflation due to excess printing of fiat capital. A great example is Venezuela, where their levels of inflation have exceeded 1 million percent (and still rising). Their currency is worthless. Holding onto it will dramatically reduce your net worth in a very short period of time. Venezuelans do not want to be paid in their national bolívar currency, rather in commodities, dollars or… **bitcoin.**

Yep, bitcoin. The demand for bitcoin in Venezuela has skyrocketed, increasing month on month despite the cryptocurrency market being in a downtrend. Can we use this as evidence that during times of fear, people may in fact flock to cryptos? Very possibly.

What I find even more interesting is the Venezuelan government has released a cryptocurrency called the "petro" which is backed by the country's oil and mineral reserves. This cryptocurrency was created for two purposes: one, to replace the plummeting bolívar and two, to surpass US sanctions and access international trade and financial markets. To cut a long story short, this seemed like a desperate cash grab from a very desperate government, rather than a revolutionary shift in finance in Venezuela. The initial idea was imposed in December, during the bull rally of 2017. As Venezuelans were filled with fear, the opportunity of cryptocurrencies seemed too good to turn down. The US did not like the idea of the petro dollar and stated that they would be violating US sanctions because it "would appear to be an extension of credit to the Venezuelan government".

I honestly don't know how this is going to turn out. The public sale starts next month, and there are many concerns. My largest concern is that the US will retaliate with force. The US like control, and crypto assets take this control away from them. Russia has apparently helped Venezuela avoid sanctions and set up this crypto asset. They deny these claims – however, out of the four methods of purchasing the Petro tokens, three were cryptocurrencies and the final option was Russian rubles. If Russia is supporting Venezuela, and the US try to go to use force or impose tariffs, we could see Russia stepping in.

The second major concern I have is that there is no proof that the petro is actually backed by anything, and is just a cash grab. Time will tell how this play out. What an interesting time to be alive!

Venezuela is a great case study to show that during times of fear, people are quick to change. The combination of the extremely high trading volume for cryptocurrencies from retail investors and the government involvement to try and create a commodity-backed crypto asset is great evidence that a similar scenario can play out if hyperinflation or a recession occurs in the wider economy.

The second biggest argument that cryptocurrencies will be adopted during a crisis is the fact that, for the first time ever, it presents an alternative to currency that isn't controlled by the banks/governments. It's safe to say fewer and fewer people are trusting banks, especially after the 2008 financial crisis. If a financial crisis happens, and many people experience significant financial difficulties as a result, they very much may shift to an alternative.

Unfortunately, this is the most likely scenario for quick mass adoption. People are lazy, and will only act when they absolutely have to. Fear is a very powerful emotion, and gets people to act. We already have a strong foundation of investors in the cryptocurrency space who strongly dislike banks (to put it nicely), so it is inevitable during a crisis that these investors will be able to easily convert those on the fence into the space and trigger a domino effect and rapidly progress adoption.

We've covered that cryptos can very well be used as an uncorrelated asset during a financial crisis. Institutional investors may consider having a small allocation towards the cryptocurrency market and retail investors will likely follow the herd. We've also mentioned that during times of extreme fear and desperation, change happens. People will be more inclined to shift to crypto assets once they feel the repercussions of the corrupt banking system.

Against Crypto Assets

In light of keeping this a fair argument, I will highlight a few points as to why cryptos may not perform well during a financial crisis. The first point is that cryptos have never been exposed to a financial crisis, so why would investors pour their hard-earned capital into a market that has never been exposed to such an event? It is a huge risk and institutional capital is much more likely to stick with what they know than explore an unknown asset class during times of despair. I think this is a very fair statement to make – however, I know if the crypto markets are picking up while other markets are falling, human nature will cause the fear of missing out to lure those who are sceptical about the market in.

The second main argument I hear is that investors are scared of the cryptocurrency market. A significant number of crypto investors got in during the 2017 December rally, right at the top. These investors have experienced significant losses and have likely shared their stories to all of their connections. These investors will be very scep-tical about investing in the market, and until the crypto-currency market reaches all-time highs, they are unlikely to invest again. That's what got them in the market in the first place, also why they lost a lot of money.

To conclude, no-one knows how crypto assets will perform during a financial crisis. However, we have seen how countries that are in financial ruin are widely invest-ing in crypto assets and integrating the technology into their fiscal and monetary policies. Only time will tell, but my best bet is that they will perform extremely well.

The Greater Fool Theory

The greater fool theory is the act of purchasing an asset with the assumption that someone else (the greater fool) will purchase it at a higher price. Bill Gates apparently said that Bitcoin is this type of investment.

To put it simply, I buy bitcoin assuming that you will buy it at a higher price. That's the greater fool theory.

The truth is that all asset classes will have this element to them, as markets are run by fear and greed. Why do people buy stocks when their P/E ratios are extremely overvalued? Because they expect the market to continue rising. Why does the real estate market keep on rising, despite the average income to the average property price reaching all-time highs? Because investors expect the price to keep on rising.

The "bitcoin bubble" is often compared to the tulip bubble that started in 1636 and rose over 6000% in a number of years. The tulip bubble was when tulips were brought into Holland from Turkey and the Dutch loved the novelty of this new, rare flower. They were buying bulbs, which are exclusive rights to use an entire strain of tulip. As it takes about 10 years for a bulb to form from seed, there was a huge element of scarcity in this market.

As different colours and patterns of this flower emerged into the Dutch market, it became a fashion statement to own such rare bulbs. In simple economic terms, the rarity of the bulbs (supply) was significantly over-weighed by the demand of the Dutch society, and got to the point where people were selling their houses, land and life savings for a flower! Why would they do such a thing? Because they believed that the tulip price would forever rise. Hence, the fear of missing out on a potential profit lead the whole nation into believing that a flower was worth more than a house.

This is the greater fool theory.

The expectation of higher prices leads investors, both retail and institutional, to continue to buy an asset far beyond the underlying value. Of course, it is very hard to define an underlying value for bitcoin and other cryptocurrencies. They are often referred to as "worthless digital coins". However, this could not be further from the truth. They represent a paradigm shift in trust from centralization to decentralization. Crypto assets also represent the next phase of value exchange. Throughout history money has evolved, from barter, to gold and silver, to fiat capital. With each evolution, it has become faster and more convenient for the wider market to transact. Distributed ledger technology is the next step, and it is coming after the traditional banking sector and every middleman business out there.

Distributed ledger technology (DLT) is here to stay.

Investors in the cryptocurrency market are early adopters; the user interface and technology are nowhere near ready for mass adoption at the moment (they are the greater fools). The process of buying and securing digital assets is far too complicated for the average person to figure out, and the risks of being hacked or scammed are huge for both retail and institutional investors.

That's why **now** is the best time to get in. Before it becomes as simple as clicking "buy the market" on an app where your cryptos are insured and stored for you. Before these projects start to steal market share from every sector out there. Before everyone else is getting in. It's kind of like during the mid-90s, when the early adopters started investing in Internet stocks. It starts off with the "crazy" people, the tech nerds, the punters, those "in the know" etc.… and then word spreads to the early adopters. People who might be actively invested in other asset classes/technologies and are constantly on the lookout for new opportunities, and of course institutional investors start to eye up technologies at this point. Once they have the same epiphany as the very early adopters, they then spread the message down the grapevine and the institutional investors build financial products to capitalize on the emerging technology.

The tech bubble eventually burst during the process of "commercialisation", which was around a market capitalization of $5 trillion USD (taking inflation into account). Commercialisation is just another way of saying when the general public adopted and widely invested in the technology.

People drive markets, and emotions drive people. Fear and greed determine which direction any market will be moving. Once the power of DLTs clicks with a newer investor and they realise the potential it will have on the global economy, they become very bullish on crypto assets.

But, being an early adopter, we have to navigate through the difficulties of an emerging market. Just like during the 90s when the Internet started to gain traction but had to overcome several similar hurdles to gain mass adoption. I'm sure you remember having to get off the Internet when someone in your house needed to use the phone. Or waiting ages for a simple webpage to load. This is where we are in the crypto space.

I speak about knowing when to sell in later chapters. However, understanding that every single person in this market is essentially buying with the hope of someone buying at a higher price will help you massively when the mass public enters the market (that's a good exit signal).

Remember, if you invest in this market, you are looking for a return on your investment (ROI). Don't believe anyone that claims they're in it for the technology – they're not. As an investor, getting a good ROI is your only priority! If you really only care about the technology, you can always be charitable to these projects. This may seem pretty ruthless, but the reality is that 95% of these crypto projects are rubbish, and will fail. I do not want anyone having the mentality that most investors in this market have. Do not fall in love with ANY crypto. Know that before this market matures, we will see wild speculation and the greater fool's theory will be in full effect. If you are ignorant of this theory, then you may be the greater fool.

Confirmation Bias

Confirmation bias is poison. This is the biggest reason why people just "hold" their way to the bottom and never capitalise on any gains or hold on to losing investments, waiting for them to skyrocket.

What is confirmation bias? It's when you only seek information that agrees with your point of view. This is extremely dangerous and very hard to avoid. You will always have some level of confirmation bias within you – it's human nature. We want to be right, and hate admitting when we are wrong. Guess what? The market does not care about your opinion. Let me repeat that because it is so important…

The market does not care about YOUR opinion.

Many investors get trapped in communities that are created around an individual crypto; do you really think you'll get balanced opinions in there? It is very important to follow a few sources that have completely opposite points of view to you and judge them from a neutral standpoint. Understand exactly what and why they are saying it. I follow several investors who HATE cryptocurrencies, and I completely understand where they are coming from in many respects. I don't agree with what they are saying most of the time, but at least I am aware. I always consider the reasons not to invest in an asset class or individual asset before investing. In fact, I consider this the most important phase of due diligence. Find someone that disagrees with you, find the facts and evaluate your decision from a neutral standpoint. This alone has saved me thousands of pounds. Right before I was about to jump into a project because of the fear of missing out (FOMO), I would make sure to seek alternative viewpoints on that project, and I would often see red flags that have stopped me investing in many projects (thankfully).

When you form an opinion on something, you steer away from the unbiased facts, and twist information to match what you are thinking. Sometimes your belief will be right, and you'll feel great. Just know that you will be wrong, and sometimes it is better to accept the fact that you are wrong and cut your losses short than to try and wait to prove that you are right. Trust me, I've lost a lot of money in the past trying to do this. Being stubborn will only lose you money!

The Power of Your Mind

Trading emotionally has by far caused me to lose the most money in the shortest period of time. You need to be ruthlessly emotionless when investing and trading. You need to be as disciplined as a Navy Seal and as patient as your spouse (lol) when it comes to placing and monitoring trades.

This is much easier said than done.

As you're investing your hard-earned capital, you will always have some level of emotional connection to it. Which is fine, as long as you don't let your emotions control you. The most common way your emotions will sabotage you are:

- Buying a crypto after it has just rallied massively
- Selling near a bottom as there is mass panic
- Following the crowd (search "emergent norm theory")

Have you bought near the top? Sold near a bottom? Bought a coin just because everyone else is? I have, I've done all three, several times. Before I was aware as to why this kept on happening, I used to blame the market, or blame the market manipulators. The reality is, it was entirely MY fault. No-one else's. You need to take 100% responsibility for all of your trades, whether up or down. Justifications are simply your ego avoiding being wrong, which a lot of the time, you will be. I would much rather make a profit than be right. There have been several times when I have publicly stated a trade, to then realise I am wrong, and instantly change my positioning. Chasing perfection is an illusion.

This is why people just "hold", or buy near the top and wait for the price to continue rallying. The number one rule of trading is to cut your losses short and let your profits run. If you are wrong, accept it, take the small loss and move on. Manipulators profit immensely from emotional investors; they know exactly how to cause an emotional reaction in the masses, and use the media and large amounts of capital to ensure their move.

These five tips will significantly help you control your emotions when trading/investing…

1. **Risk capital**

This isn't the first nor the last time I will mention this. Do not invest more money than you are willing to lose. The question I ask when adding more capital is, "If I lost all of this money, would I be in S#@%?" If yes, then I will reduce the amount until I am comfortable. If no, then go ahead.

Also, a lot of investors in the crypto markets only invest in crypto assets. This is very risky and can seriously hurt your long-term financial goals. I am not a financial advisor, but good allocations to the crypto market range from 5-20% dependent on risk tolerance, age and whether you are looking to aggressively accumulate wealth, or preserve it.

If you have money you can afford to lose, it makes trading a lot easier. I have heard some pretty depressing stories about people losing everything due to going all in on crypto assets. Please don't let this happen to you.

2. **Limit how often you trade**

I only look at the charts **three times a day**: once in the morning, once at midday and once in the evening. The total time I spend doing so is around 30 minutes.

I used to spend hours every single day looking at the charts and at CoinMarketCap. This was unhealthy, and was against my values. I'm investing for time and freedom, not to be a slave to the charts.

This is actually a serious issue; the markets are addictive and they are 24/7. If you find you can't help but look at the charts every hour, then maybe you need to seek help. There are several treatment centres open specifically for cryptocurrency addicts.

This will also help you avoid the fear of missing out (FOMO) and not get sucked into small intraday moves.

Three times may be too much for you, and once a week may suffice. I look frequently because I'm a full-time investor/trader and have the time/ability to do so.

3. **Take a walk**

This may seem very weird, and if I was reading this when I first started, I would never have done it. I've lost a lot of money rushing into trades in the past, especially those I was uncertain of or those purely made due to emotions. Now, I take a walk and wait a few hours before placing the trade. You don't have to take a walk, just do something else to let your emotions settle down and then make a rational decision.

This tip alone will save you thousands.

I've placed trades, then taken a walk to think over it, only to realise that I was either overexposing myself or just completely wrong. When you remove your ego and emotions from the picture, it can help you place risk-adjusted trades that are far more likely to go in your favour.

4. **Ask a friend**

This is normally a secondary method for me. When I am not sure, or when I want a second opinion on a trade, I will reach out to a few trading friends to see what they have to say. I mostly do this to avoid confirmation bias, but also to see what their opinion is. Sometimes they agree, and also take the trade and profit (which is great). Other times, they disagree, and point out some flaws, which helps me save capital. Sure, there will be times when it is very 50/50 – you just need to make your own decision and learn from it if you are wrong, and to call them up and ask why they thought differently to you.

You're probably thinking, "Well, Devin, I don't have any trading friends…" which may be true right now, but you have to start somewhere. I had zero connections when I first started in this market, but I reached out and shared my opinions and eventually I had many people both supporting my views and going against them, which was and still is great.

To begin with, you can email me and I'll be more than happy to provide some feedback.

5. **Take your initial investment out**

The sense of relief when I did this was amazing. Once you do this, you'll have nothing to lose. When your portfolio doubles, take your initial investment out. Yes, with the investment in, it could go a lot higher, but it could also go down massively. This is more for your peace of mind than anything else.

The Six Suckers

Before we dive into the secrets, I want to share a few stories that led me to discover these secrets. I lost a lot of capital learning these lessons, but I am glad that I did. I urge you to leverage my experience, and not make the same mistakes that I did when I first started out (I made many!).

#001 Buying at peaks

I first entered the market at the start of 2017, right after the Q4 rally that cryptos tend to have. I did not know this at the time, and bought BTC at all-time highs, around $1,200 USD. It then fell, and I immediately lost 30% of my original investment. This was due to a lack of patience and overwhelming excitement I had to get in the market. The loss didn't annoy me that much; it was the fact that I could have got an additional 0.5 BTC by just waiting a couple weeks. Had I looked at the charts and taken some time to analyze the market trend, I may have waited, or at least averaged in. So yeah, that stung. But I learnt a lot from it! I think everyone has experienced this a few times in the cryptocurrency market.

#002 Selling at bottoms

Unfortunately, when I first started out and didn't know that much, I let my emotions take control of my investments. Buying at highs, selling near lows. Looking back, I was an absolute novice. I remember selling bitcoin at $1,000 after it rallied and then came crashing down; I then had to rebuy at $1,100. I had a really bad start, and I learnt a tremendous amount from these lessons (the secrets will cover these in great detail).

#003 Buying news

It took me months to figure this out – I just didn't understand why. One project I was in announced that they had a partnership announcement coming soon. I was very excited and watched closely for this announcement, a couple weeks later it came and I rushed to buy it, and guess what happened? The price plummeted. I was dumbfounded. The announcement was good, so why did the price fall? I'll cover this in great detail later, as it is one of the most vital lessons you will ever learn.

#004 ICOs

I invested in so many lucrative ICOs, they seemed like a no-brainer and everyone else was investing in them. I made sure to do my due diligence on the projects, and I did a thorough job. However, the vital factor I left out was how the ICO was structured, which I later learned was a recipe for my financial ruin.

#005 Following traders

Every "expert" out there I've likely followed and studied. Unfortunately, most of them are just great at marketing, yet have very little market knowledge. I remember following a call from a trader who was absolutely sure that x coin was about to skyrocket, so I bought it, and it dumped. This wasn't some random trader; it was a well-known influencer in the cryptocurrency space. I've learnt a lot about cryptocurrency influencers and all I can say is that there are the good (few), the bad and the ugly. Again, I'll speak about this in detail in later chapters.

#006 Trading with emotions

This is by far the biggest mistake that I have made investing/trading in this market. When you have skin in the game, you are emotionally invested as well. I used to let the wild fluctuations in the market control my mood. It was really unhealthy and I lost a lot of money by trading when I was tired, sad, confused, overexcited, angry. When you have other things on your mind, you make mistakes. I have made many errors with even basic technical analysis due to my mind not being in the right place.

This one takes a while to get good at controlling, and even still there are times when my emotions get the better of me. I wouldn't let this one get to you too much; we're human, after all!

21 Crypto Secrets

That Turned 4 Figures Into 6 Figures in Less Than 12 Months

Secret 1: Bitcoin Dominance

This secret is very controversial, and the purpose is not to debate whether bitcoin is the future of money or a store of value, rather to argue that bitcoin may not be the best investment in certain circumstances. Your portfolio percentage allocation to bitcoin will dramatically impact your overall percentage return. It is the difference between a 300% return and a 1000% return.

To begin, let's have a quick look at the history of Bitcoin and distributed ledger technology (DLT) in order to understand why I believe that having a heavily weighted portfolio towards bitcoin will dramatically reduce your return on your investment (ROI) going forward.

Bitcoin was revealed shortly after the 2008 financial crisis and presented the first global alternative to government-controlled fiat currency in history. However, the only people that really knew of Bitcoin back then were cryptographers, as the Bitcoin whitepaper was posted in a cryptography forum. Bitcoin inspired many talented developers to create, improve and evolve this powerful technology at such a rapid pace. If it were not for Bitcoin, we would not have seen DLTs surface for years to come.

Fast forward a few years and the first alternative crypto assets were created off the back of Bitcoin's source code, these assets are commonly referred to as "altcoins". As developers kept on tweaking and changing the code and different approaches arose, more altcoins were created. The side effect of innovation is often disruption, and those that can vision the future of crypto assets have skyrocketed the competition within the cryptocurrency space.

Bitcoin was just the beginning.

Now in 2018, we have over 1,800 different projects aiming to disrupt many markets in many different ways. This is no longer a group of developers on a cryptography forum playing with this exciting new concept. This is the Wild West racing to steal market share from global corporations that are turning their backs to this technology. Those who try to ignore this wave of innovation will be sitting ducks – especially middlemen.

Here are the three main reasons why bitcoin will lose its market share over time and why altcoins will significantly outperform bitcoin during bullish trends.

1) Percentage return to date

Bitcoin's price originally was worth less than $1/10^{th}$ of a cent. That's $0.001 USD per BTC. At the time of writing, bitcoin's most recent peak was near $20K. That's a return near 20 million percent. Now, not many people bought at these levels, as there wasn't much volume or interest. Most super early adopters bought around the $100 range, which would still make it a 20,000% ROI. The point I am driving across is that bitcoin has had the majority of its growth; don't let bigger numbers deceive true return on investment. For example, if bitcoin goes from $10K to $20K, the ROI would only be 100%. This may seem like a significant return, but if you factor in the necessary increase in market cap that is needed, this return isn't as impressive.

Which leads nicely to point 2…

2) Bitcoin's market cap is HUGE and more importantly, it makes up for more than 50%* of the entire market!

With the introduction of so many alternative cryptocurrencies, bitcoin is going to struggle to maintain such a high dominance. Before 2017, bitcoin held strongly above 80%. During 2017, this dropped to the low 40% levels and in 2018, we have seen bitcoin's dominance fall to the mid 30% levels a few times now.

Remember that one of the reasons for bitcoin's dominance being so high was due to the first mover advantage, the lack of competition/infancy of DLT and being one of the only coins with sufficient volume to facilitate bigger transaction sizes.

My prediction is that bitcoin's dominance will fall as low as 25% during the next proper rally. As the market cap continues to climb, bitcoin's dominance will continue to fall, potentially settling around the 10% level over a longer period of time.

The third and final reason why I believe bitcoin's dominance will continue to fall over time is due to…

3) Trading pair dominance

In order to buy cryptocurrencies other than bitcoin, historically, you had to buy bitcoin first and then send your bitcoin over to an altcoin exchange where you could trade your bitcoin for altcoins. Put simply, you could not buy altcoins without first owning bitcoin. This is why we often see bitcoin pick up first, and then altcoins rally soon after.

In 2016, some exchanges opened Ethereum markets, meaning you could now purchase altcoins with Ethereum instead of bitcoin. While this had a small impact on bitcoin's overall reliance as a trading pair, most people still chose to use BTC as they tend to have far larger volume. In 2017 a coin called Tether came in as a third trading pair, with the advantage of being pegged to the dollar (supposedly). Whilst Tether seems like a great alternative trading pair, the transparency behind the auditing of Tether has scared many investors from using it.

Going forward, altcoin exchanges are going to be introducing fiat trading pairs (USD, EUR, GBP etc.) and this will completely remove the need to initially buy bitcoin. There is a selection of higher cap coins which you can buy without bitcoin at the moment, but most still rely on owning bitcoin first. Once there is no need to own bitcoin before you can own altcoins, the reliance of bitcoin as a trading pair will fall dramatically.

To conclude, bitcoin has already increased a tremendous amount since its inception. That's not to say it won't increase further – it likely will. But with the removal of the need to own bitcoin before owning altcoins and with bitcoin already having such a huge market cap, bitcoin is likely to increase by a much smaller percentage than many altcoins out there.

So, back to your portfolio allocation. In a bullish market, diversifying into altcoins will significantly increase your overall return on your investment compared to just holding bitcoin. A lot of early adopters are very emotionally connected to bitcoin, and as mentioned earlier, being emotionally connected to any investment can seriously damage your potential returns and also lose you a lot of money.

So, I've mentioned that having a heavily weighted portfolio during a bullish market will limit your overall return, but what do you do during a bearish trend?

Secret 2: Bitcoin Is KING

Now before I sound like I am contradicting myself, bitcoin will limit your returns in a trending bull market. However, in a bear market, bitcoin is KING (at the moment).

As mentioned before, in order to purchase altcoins presently, you need to buy bitcoin first, and then buy whichever altcoins. So, the process looks like this…

FIAT – **BTC** – ALTCOIN

During bear markets, fear is high and many investors (especially newer ones) panic sell. anticipating further falling. Whilst the markets are falling and during times of uncertainty, we often see people hovering in the mid-section of the altcoin transaction process as mentioned before. To put it clearly, investors sit in bitcoin, as they can swiftly move in either direction, based on where the market moves.

This is why we often see bitcoin's dominance rapidly climbing during bearish trends/retracements and equally why we see bitcoin's dominance fall when the markets are looking bullish.

There are two reasons why bitcoin is seen as king during times of uncertainty and in bearish trends.

1) Percentage loss

Put simply, bitcoin loses less percentage-wise compared to altcoins when the market drops. Early 2018 was a great example of this. Bitcoin's all-time high (ATH) was around $20K and subsequently fell to just below $6K very briefly a few times this year. This drop is fairly significant at just over 70% from its ATH. However, if you compare this with many altcoins, this is a far smaller loss.

Here's a list of the largest altcoins that follow bitcoin in terms of market cap and their percentage loss, from their ATH to their 2018 low (figures are rounded for ease):

Coin	ATH	2018 Low*	Percentage Loss
BTC	$20K	$6K	70%
ETH	$1,400	$270	80%
XRP	$3.65	$0.27	90%
BCC	$4,100	$490	90%
EOS	$22	$4.40	80%
XLM	$0.9	$0.175	80%

*August 2018

As you can see, bitcoin fell almost 10% less than the other heavy cap coins and the reality is that the smaller cap coins took a much heavier fall, some over 95%.

The difference between -70% and -80% might not seem like a lot, but it makes a huge difference once the markets turn around again. Here's a simple explanation…

Bob lost 80% of a $1,000 portfolio, leaving him with $200.
Jane lost 70% of an equal $1,000 portfolio, leaving her with $300.

In order for Bob to return to the $1,000 level, he will need an overall return of 500%!
HOWEVER: in order for Jane to return to break even, she will only need a 334% return.

This is one of the perks of owning bitcoin during a bearish trend. You will lose less than the market average and therefore it will be easier to recuperate losses down the line.

1) Initial BTC rally

The second reason goes back to my earlier point in regards to the process of purchasing altcoins. Here's a reminder…

FIAT – BTC – ALTCOINS

After a downturn bitcoin's dominance is almost always at relative highs which reflects the uncertainty of the market – people want to be in BTC if the market continues falling (as mentioned above). However, they do not want to miss out, in case the market suddenly reverses, which it has done many times historically.

During this waiting period, we often see investors that are completely sitting on the sidelines start to average in. As highlighted above, they have to buy bitcoin first before they can rebuy altcoins and they also choose to buy bitcoin first to mitigate the risk of the market further falling. This causes both the market cap to rise and also the price of bitcoin, normally by a greater percentage than most altcoins.

This process normally unfolds over the course of a couple weeks. However, this ranges between 1-4 weeks and then the capital is shifted to altcoins and we see bitcoin's dominance drop massively.

Secret 3: Fork It

Forks sound very complicated but all they are essentially is a change in the rules of a cryptocurrency. Think of hundreds of people walking down a road and the road comes to a fork; some people may decide that they do not want to follow the traditional direction of the masses and take the other route—as they believe it to be better. This would split the crowd and others may follow. In terms of cryptocurrency, the minority of followers would create a new coin (think of Bitcoin Gold, Bitcoin Cash, Bitcoin Private etc.).

There are two types of forks. However, we will be focussing on hard forks as they are where significant money can be made. To begin, let's quickly summarise the difference between a hard and a soft fork…

Soft forks are quite common. In the rare case when two or more miners validate a block of transactions at the same time, they will each produce their own hash (verification code) for that block. This often gets resolved as the next block is added to the blockchain, and then the computers that process the transactions can verify that this chain is the longest and most valid chain, rendering the other chain invalid.
Put simply, when bundles of transactions are confirmed at the same time by two computers that verify transactions, a soft fork is created and then the longest chain of the following blocks of transactions will become the legitimate chain.

Hard forks (our focus) are intentional and are imposed by the developers of the crypto project or by the wider developer community, which is often the case for open source projects. The developers impose a hard fork to change the rules of the blockchain that the coin operates on. Bitcoin's code is open source; therefore, developers can put forward potential changes at any time.

There are two ways a hard fork can go:

1. (The most common.) The majority of nodes do not agree with the new rules and continue as normal. If the fork occurs and a percentage of nodes do follow the new rules, the majority will reject their blocks and force them to create their own cryptocurrency (take Bitcoin Gold, for example).
2. The majority of nodes agree with the change in rules and the nodes that run the existing rules are forced to either change rules, or they fork off and create a new cryptocurrency (see below).

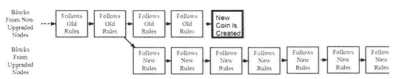

A Hard Fork: Non-Upgraded Nodes Reject The New Rules, Diverging The Chain

Put simply, a hard fork is a change of rules and those who disagree with the majority will have to create their own cryptocurrency off of the back of the origin coin's code.

The reason why hard forks are worth monitoring is that when a new token is created, the holders of the origin token receive a certain amount of the new token just by holding the origin token, either from supporting exchanges or in the designated wallet.

Leading up to the hard fork, we often see the price of the origin asset increase a significant amount. This is mostly due to investors wanting to receive "free cash" as soon as the split occurs. Below is the step-by-step guide detailing how this process works, and how to profit from it. I'll be using a previous Bitcoin hard fork as an illustration.

1. Hard fork is announced.

Bitcoin Gold announced its hard fork early on in October 2017.

At this point, you want to either purchase the origin asset or move your existing holdings of this coin into a wallet/exchange that supports the fork.

2. The price of the origin asset (Bitcoin, in this case) rises, leading up to the fork date.

Bitcoin rose from the low $4K levels at the beginning of October to the $6K levels in just a few weeks before the fork occurred. Of course, this climb in price was not entirely due to investors buying BTC purely for this fork, but it was a driving factor.

You have two options at this point. Your first option is to sell the origin asset at a profit a few days before the fork. You will most likely make a good profit from doing so. However, you will miss out on the new token and the value from it. Your second option would come after step 3…

3. The price of both the origin asset and the newly created coin plummet.

Bitcoin dropped over 10% on the same day that the hard fork occurred, which is a sharp drop in a trending bull market. However, the significant fall is almost always in the newly created coin. In this case, Bitcoin Gold dropped over 75% on the day of the fork. As a side note, Bitcoin Gold has now dropped over 95% since the fork.

Your second option is to sell both the origin asset and the new token as soon as the snapshot* has occurred. This is what most people do, but the problem is that with most people selling, it is easy for your market sell order to not fill. Setting a sell order below market price increases the likelihood of your order filling.

The pros of selling as soon as the snapshot occurs are that you will have prevented the temporary drop in the price of the origin asset and also acquired a holding of this new token. The value of the new token is often unknown upon release. As an example, Bitcoin Gold was initially priced near $400 per token. I don't think many people would complain about being given $400 for free!

The third option which I did not mention above is to simply hold the origin asset in a supporting wallet/exchange and then just hold through the fork and hope the value of both the origin asset and the newly created token increase over time. This is also what a lot of people do, but it is certainly not the most profitable avenue. Most newly forked coins tend to lose a lot of value immediately and (dependant on the market trend) struggle to return back to this level.

Hard forks are usually announced a few months before the snapshot and most of the price activity occurs within the final two weeks leading up to the hard fork. To maximise the potential ROI, it is best to get into the origin asset three to four weeks before the hard fork (I expect this to become longer over time).

* The snapshot is when the blocks are split and the new coin is created – the easiest way to find out when this is for a particular token is to just google it.

Secret 4: The Binance Effect

This secret is not exclusive to just Binance. However, Binance is well known for this. Other large exchanges also have a similar impact. The exchanges that will have an even greater impact will be larger volume exchanges... Coinbase and Kraken, for example.

What is "The Binance Effect"?

At its core, the introduction of a new crypto to an exchange usually causes an immediate spike in the price of that crypto. Exchanges like Binance offer a significantly higher level of volume to newer projects that are listed. This is the first major reason why new projects skyrocket as soon as they are listed on Binance. However, the second and most important reason is that the vast majority of crypto investors have a Binance account and many people immediately buy the token upon listing, expecting a spike in price. Investors also often purchase the coin on other exchanges in anticipation of it being listed on Binance.

There aren't many ways of predicting which coins will be listed on Binance or other exchanges other than the official announcements from the exchanges themselves. You can rigorously follow the development teams of many projects, and question whether or not they have submitted a proposal to large volume exchanges, but note that they share the status of the proposal due to insider trading laws. If they have submitted it, the probability is obviously much higher than if not.

Here are two things to keep in mind that will help you choose coins with a much greater probability of being listed on high-volume exchanges:

- Binance charges a fairly significant fee to be listed on their exchange, so smaller cap coins stand almost no change unless there is a community vote for them.
- Binance thoroughly tests the code of the project, and doesn't tend to let joke coins on their exchange. I expect the same for all high-volume exchanges.

Community Voting

Other than paying a significant fee to be listed on Binance, a token can also be added via community voting. There is normally a selection of coins that the wider Binance community vote for to be listed on the exchange during the next month. During the voting period, it is quite common to see the price of the leading coin(s) increase a significant amount. This is simply the market pricing in the Binance effect before it happens, so when the coin is listed on the exchange, the price will likely rise less or even fall, due to the market already pricing in the listing (there are other variables, but this is a major one). It is important to keep an eye out on the community voting and get in the favourable coins earlier in the voting process rather than later and be cautious that the price may fall upon listing.

To summarise, if the coin is known to be listed on a high-volume exchange in the near future, the price will increase, leading up to the listing and then fall on the day, as the market has already priced in the listing.

If the coin is listed as a surprise then there will likely be a significant short-term spike in the price of that coin, and then the direction of the price going forward will be determined by the market. The reason why I say this is due to the fact that in bear markets there is often a spike, but then the coin will fall in price over the next couple of weeks, simply following the market trend.

Always remember the foundational rule – buy the rumour, sell the news.

Secret 5: Market Cap

The next three secrets cover common misconceptions about market capitalization, price and the psychological impact that price has.

To begin, let's define market capitalization.

Put simply, market capitalization is the price of an individual crypto asset multiplied by the circulating supply of that asset. It is worth noting that the circulating supply is a variable and will more than likely increase over time. I've created a maths triangle to help you calculate this going forward.

Figure 1.0 The Crypto Triangle

1. Price x Circulating Supply = Market Cap
2. Circulating Supply/Market Cap = Price
3. Market Cap/Price = Circulating Supply

One of the biggest confusions people have is that the market cap reflects the actual dollar value that has been invested in the asset. This is completely incorrect; the real number is far lower. However, this is good news as it requires far less capital to move the cryptocurrency markets than one thinks.

Let me explain.

Bitcoin is priced at $10,000 USD with a circulating supply of 17 million.

Using the triangle provided earlier, we can calculate the market cap by multiplying the price by the circulating supply.

$10,000 USD x 17,000,000 = $170 billion USD.

Suddenly the price of bitcoin shoots up to $11,000 USD, making the market cap 187 billion – an increase of 17 billion to the market cap. This is where many people assume that $17 billion has just been added to the market, which is wrong.

In a buyers and sellers' market, there needs to be sufficient sell volume to fill large bitcoin buy orders. In other words, there needs to be a seller to match the buyer's request. If there is no seller at that price point, the price will increase until there is sufficient volume to fill larger orders.

Where there is an imbalance, there is a reactionary movement in price in the market. When the market is bullish, there is a greater percentage of buyers than sellers, hence the price continues to rise. In a bearish market this the opposite, sellers outweigh buyers and therefore cause the price to plummet.

If I am buying $10 million worth of bitcoin at $10,000 USD, there needs to be sufficient selling volume at that price level to fill my order. If there is not, then the price will increase until my order is filled. So, a relatively small amount (compared to 17 billion) of $10 million can cause the market cap to climb by a much higher perceived dollar value than the actual investment. $10 million is more likely to move the price up by a couple hundred dollars. However, the effect on market cap would still be in the billions.

Now we understand that market cap is not a true reflection of the amount of capital in the market, let's talk about the more important metric… volume!

(By the way, I've put this calculator into a tool that you can use online. Go to www.cryptotools.co.uk to get access to it.)

Secret 6: Volume

Pump and dump schemes thrive off of low volume cryptocurrencies, as they are the easiest to manipulate and pump the price.

Let me explain why volume is more important than market cap, and how easy it is to manipulate the market cap.

Taking it back to Figure 1.0, we know that market cap is determined by multiplying price by circulating supply. Here's an example of how this is manipulated.

I and my hypothetical evil twin Kevin create our own coin, called PUMP coin. There are 100 tokens in circulation, and we own 99 of them. The other token we manage to get listed on a small exchange. I initially buy that token for $100, setting a market value for the token.

The market cap is now perceived as $100 USD x 100 tokens = $10,000 USD.

Now, in order to manipulate market cap and get uninformed investors to buy PUMP coin, I set a sell order at $1,000 USD and my evil twin Kevin buys it. Now the market cap is $1,000 USD x 100 tokens = $100,000 USD and has a total percentage increase of 1,000% in such a short period of time.

The rapid increase in price will draw many eyes to this asset and many investors will try to "ride the wave" while this token is increasing.

Kevin and I sit patiently, waiting for the ~~idiot~~ investors chasing this high return. We have a sell order for all 100 of our tokens set at the market price, which is $1,000 USD.

All of a sudden, there are 10 buy orders at market price, and we very happily fill them.

We now have $10,000 USD from the investors, and the investors – well they have 10 PUMP tokens.

Now, when those investors go to sell, there will not be any volume to sell to. They've all bought at $1,000 USD, so they don't want to sell at that level. But no-one is buying PUMP coin at that level. So, what happens? The price plummets to a level at which there is sufficient buying volume so those investors can sell – which may never come. A lot of investors I have spoken to have fallen for this trap, and been forced to remain in coins like this due to extremely low volume.

Secret 6 – don't buy into low volume coins. Your orders will not fill and there is a possibility of you being trapped in that token until the volume picks up again (if ever).

This has happened to me many times before, and is a costly lesson to learn. Don't be fooled by the pump and dump schemes that amateurs comment on… "x coin has increased 600% today" and then you go to see that there is less than $10,000 USD volume.

Aim for at least $100,000 USD volume over a 24-hour period, and you know that your order (assuming it is under $5K) will likely fill at or near market price. You can use www.coinmarketcap.com to check the 24hr volume for all assets.

Before we move on, another really important lesson that doesn't warrant an entire chapter but fits nicely here is slippage.

Slippage is essentially when the price of an asset moves further in a particular direction than originally intended. For example, if you go to sell a large amount of BTC at market price (let's say this is $11K) and there is not sufficient volume at that price point, the price you sell at will fall (or "slip") to a level where there is sufficient volume to fill your order. This works for both buying and selling.

This has happened to me countless times before. This is far more common with altcoins, and the lower the volume, the more common this will become. I have had times where I have tried to buy at really low-price levels just for the price to be massively moved upwards, due to a relatively large purchase amount (compared to the 24hr volume). So, it turns out that some of that purchase will fill at that low-price level but a lot of it will fill higher. You will also notice when you try and sell at market high levels that you might get your order partially filled at the high level and then the rest at a lower level.

The easiest way to avoid this is to place limit sell/buy orders to make sure your trade will only be executed at these levels. However, the downside to this is that your order might not entirely get filled. There have been times when I just want to get into the market, so I've taken a fractional loss by placing a market order rather than a limit and waiting for the volume to fill my order.

Again, this likely won't happen with high-cap, high-volume coins but is very common with many smaller alt-coins.

Secret 7: Supply

We know from the "Crypto Triangle" that supply = market cap/price. But that just scrapes the surface when it comes to supply. I believe that every investor needs to have a strong understanding of the supply of a crypto, the potential changes in supply that could happen and what is happening with the locked-up supply.

A Word of Warning

One of the biggest issues I have with many of these crypto projects is the vast amount of the overall supply that is allocated to the project. It's not uncommon to see projects that hold over 35% of the entire supply. I do see the rationale in holding tokens, for project development, team motivation, angel investing (like NEO does) and associated business costs. However, most of these projects are being run by teams who have very little experience managing a multimillion-dollar company, and they are the ones likely to rent high-end offices, travel first class globally and rack up expenses, all through the tokens that are reserved for operations. The excessive spending isn't my biggest concern – the real issue is that the lockup period for many of these projects is coming to an end. Most projects had either one or two-year lockup periods, and as most projects were created in 2017, there are only a couple months left before the teams can start shifting their tokens onto the open market.

You might be questioning what a lockup is and why it is relevant. During the crowdfunding stage (ICO), projects allocate the founders/team a percentage of the overall supply of the token. This is normally around 5% but I've seen this as high as 25% (which is ridiculous). To ease the concerns of the team just dumping their tokens on the open market as soon as the project is launched, they lock them away in a wallet which can be monitored by the community. For the past year or so, these coins have technically been in circulation but due to the lockup period, they have remained dormant. As we approach 2019, a lot of these projects will be free to sell as much of their holdings as they wish, which will crush the price of that asset.

How do we know they won't do this? I suppose all we can do is trust that they won't, and monitor the wallets closely. We're then reliant on morals and ethics, in an unregulated market that thrives off of speculation. All I'm saying is that we need to be careful of a lot of these projects whose lockup periods are now over, and are looking to cash in on the market. During September 2018, Ethereum took a massive fall. Most of this was due to the market trend as it was, but it fell by a greater amount due to all of the negative press it was getting. I was reading a few articles and came across one which stated that the reason for Ethereum's massive drop was due to a lot of the ICOs from 2017 selling off their Ether. So, it's not just the smaller projects we need to pay attention to, it's Ethereum too.

While that might all seem like doom and gloom, I do want to point out that the cryptocurrency space is centred around trust and transparency, and I expect most projects to have a high standard of ethics. However, I know some won't. Some will be greedy and try to rip off their early investors.

The other important metric we need to know about supply is a thing called "coin burns".

A coin burn can be defined as "a reduction in overall supply by sending a portion of coins to a wallet where the private key is unknown". Put simply, a coin burn is a reduction in supply. Why is this important? Let's take it back to the Crypto Triangle...

Price = Market Cap/Circulating Supply

If we reduce circulating supply, yet the market cap stays the same (as these tokens were locked up and not traded in the open market anyway), then the price of that asset goes up.

Here's a simple example...

DevinCoin

$100 USD (price), $1,000,000 (market cap), 10,000 (circulating supply)

If we decrease the circulating supply to 5,000, it would then look like this...

$1,000,000 (market cap)/5,000 (circulating supply) = $200 USD (price).

It's worth noting the impact coin burns have, and also noting that the market loves coin burns and often causes the price to rise more than the theoretical amount, due to speculation.

Secret 8: Price

The price of crypto assets varies from a fraction of a penny all the way to the high six-figure range. But what does this mean? How does the price correlate to the investment return?

One of the biggest mistakes I see is people focussing too much on the price of a certain token rather than the token itself. During the December rally, one of the most common emails I received was from people questioning what to buy as they "could not afford" bitcoin. This confused me at first, until I understood why they said it. At the time, bitcoin was trading around $10K, and many newer investors thought you had to own an entire bitcoin. With the average person investing a few thousand dollars, they were looking at alternatives to BTC to park their capital into (Secret 8 will be covering this in greater detail). This is one of the biggest mistakes I see people making: they look at price alone and nothing else.

While most people reading this book probably know that you can own a fraction of Bitcoin, the average person does not. After learning about the "Crypto Triangle", you understand how price is calculated – **Market Cap/Circulating Supply = Price** – but the average person doesn't use this calculation; they simply look at the price.

There's not much more to say on price alone, but this "secret" is so vitally important that I believe everyone needs to read it and understand that:

1) Price alone means almost nothing
2) You do not have to buy the full amount of a crypto, as most are divisible

Secret 9 will dive deeply into the psychology of price.

Secret 9: Cheapies

If there is one secret that has the most importance, it is this one. Understanding this secret will significantly impact your overall return on investment. Before we dive into the "cheapies", I want to speak about the psychological impact that price has on people.

Let me ask you a question. What would you rather have: 100,000 or 0.1?

Your answer is probably along the lines of "Of what?", am I right? I'm also assuming that despite not knowing the "what", you also probably had a slight bias towards having the 100,000.

The "what" are the tokens, such as bitcoin or Verge, which the average person knows nothing about. This is where psychology comes into play. You often get herds of people who shill* cryptocurrencies which are less than a penny, preaching about the potential of a moonshot** to $10 USD. I cringe heavily at this mentality, and the vast amount of people who actually believe this to be true. I often blame penny stocks for the miscorrelation to penny cryptos. You often hear stories of stocks that went from just a few pennies to over $10. I want to point out that when you hear about something in the news, it is there because it is an abnormal event, occurring very infrequently. Yet it has the opposite effect, people perceive this to be the norm and start pouring their capital into these penny stocks. The cryptocurrency market is no different, people like to think that their token which is currently $0.001 will eventually reach $100. Absurd.

Often people argue that bitcoin went from $0.1 all the way to near $20,000, so it is clearly possible for returns like these to happen, which I agree is possible. However, what most people fail to realise is that it was very difficult buying bitcoin at those low-price levels. There weren't many exchanges and the volume was tiny. It was only until it was around the hundred-dollar range where exchanges started to increase in volume and accessibility.

Let's say, by chance, you invested in BTC at $100. Do you really think you would have held until $20,000? My best guess is that you would have sold a lot sooner than that. Most Bitcoin millionaires either bought or mined bitcoin around 2013 and then forgot about it until last year. Over 4 million bitcoins have been lost, because back then people did not have a crystal ball so they just lost their private keys over time.

So, back to the point of owning 100,000 or 0.1. This is exactly the question many people faced in December, where their $1,000 USD could get them either 0.1 BTC or over 150,000 Verge tokens (or many others – just an example). Psychologically newer investors were drawn to Verge as they didn't want to own a fraction of a coin, and Verge was deemed a "cheapy" with massive potential.

But if we compare the performance of the two assets from the beginning of December to the end of December, you will be amazed.

Bitcoin:

1st December price = around $10,000 USD
31st December price = $14,000 USD
PEAK BTC price = $20,000 USD
ROI from the 1st to the peak = 100%

Verge:

1st December price = around $0.0055 USD
31st December price = $0.2 USD
PEAK BTC price = $0.29 USD
ROI from the 1st to the peak = over 5,000%

Using the knowledge about how people think and the psychological impact that price has on people, I was able to get in and out of 11 "cheap" coins which increased by over 1,000% in December.

The key takeaway from this chapter is that just because a crypto is "cheap" does not mean it's a good investment over a longer period of time. However, when the public comes rushing into the market, they will likely buy coins they deem as cheap. Structuring your portfolio to have some diversification to include these tokens can significantly increase your overall return. I personally like the "cheap" tokens, which are actually strong projects on their own. That way, you mitigate risk massively. But with that being said, Dogecoin (the coin named after a meme) went up 800% in December.

Remember that the only reason these tokens are "cheap" is because of the large supply not because they're undervalued.

PRICE = MARKET CAP/CIRCULATING SUPPLY

* Shill just means you promote the coin in your best interest.

** Moonshot is just a way of saying the price increasing by thousands of percent.

Secret 10: Airdrops

Let's start this chapter by defining what an airdrop is:

Google's definition: the act of dropping supplies, troops, or equipment by parachute from an aircraft

Devin's Crypto Definition: the act of dropping tokens into a user's compatible wallet

I'm heavily against the promotion of getting "free" money, as there is always a hidden agenda behind most of those schemes, and most of them are scams anyway. However, when it comes to airdrops, it often is a way to get "free" tokens. Albeit most of these tokens are worthless, occasionally you'll get the unicorn airdrop, which can be worth a serious amount of money.

I remember back in early 2018 a project called ONT gave away over 1,000 tokens just for signing up for their newsletter. I saw it at the time and just let it pass, as I had other things to do. A few months passed and ONT was finally listed on a few exchanges with a market value of… $1 USD. While this wasn't a huge figure, those 1,000 free tokens were worth over $1,000 USD. I was kicking myself for not getting involved, but not as much as when it reached $10! That was painful. The lesson learnt from this is that sometimes you may as well just sign up for these newsletters, etc., as you never know how much that token could be worth.

Here are a few tips when hunting for airdrops:

1. Don't use the same email that you use for exchanges
2. Don't ever share your private key
3. Use a separate ERC-20 compatible wallet
4. Never give out personal information (I don't trust many airdrop KYCs…)

Most of the time, in order to qualify for the free airdrop, you'll need to either subscribe to their newsletter, join their telegram community or promote some of their marketing material on your social media channel. I normally go for the ones which are newsletter/group based, as I have an email I use for spam and a telegram account that joins hundreds of random groups.

There's not much more to say about airdrops, so here are a few resources where you can find out about the upcoming airdrops:

https://airdropalert.com/ | https://airdrops.io/

The only issue I have with these sites is that they list all airdrops, without any due diligence. I am going to be creating a group where I share airdrops that I have personally done the DD for and meet my requirements. I'll be posting updates about that in the free Facebook group (feel free to join): https://www.facebook.com/groups/EMICFREECRYPTOGROUP

Secret 11: ICOS

An entire book could be written about initial coin offerings (ICOs). It is an absolutely crazy market, raising billions in funding for blockchain backed start-ups, even teams with very little or no experience. There have been countless examples of projects faking who their team was, tonnes of scammy projects and tonnes of projects that leverage the hype of the crypto space to raise money for their project that might need even need blockchain to function.

I personally tend to avoid ICOs, and I'll explain why later in this chapter. Most ICOs are projects that are built off of a platform like Ethereum or NEO and they ask for either BTC or ETH to fund their projects.

Here are the main reasons why I avoid ICOs:

1. The lock-up period

Once you send your ETH to these ICOs, it takes many months before you actually receive their token. The opportunity cost of waiting six months onwards can mean missing out on hundreds, if not thousands of percent ROI, especially during a trending bull market. This happened to me: I sent my ETH when it was around $200 to a project which I won't name, just to see ETH go to over $1,000 over the course of the next few months and I still did not receive their token. They probably capitalised on that ETH gain and then decided nine months later to send their tokens out... during the

2018 bear market. You're probably thinking,"You probably didn't do any due diligence," but I did. I read through their entire whitepaper, followed/studied their team and understood the structure of the ICO. They just took far longer than promised with the deliverability of their token, which caused me to miss out on a serious profit.

2. The structure of ICOs

Of course, not all ICOs are structured the same way. However, the vast majority follow this structure and unfortunately it hurts the little guy (us) the most. ICOs are normally done in a few rounds, you normally have a seed round, a pre-sale, then a public sale. Sometimes there are a couple more rounds, sometimes less.

Unfortunately, unless you have at least $10,000 to invest in the seed round, and you are an accredited investor, it is unlikely that you will be able to invest in the very early stages. This is what I don't like, and the reason is due to the bonus structure. Most seed rounds offer a significantly higher bonus than all other rounds – for the sake of ease, let's call this a 100% bonus.

Banker Billy decides to invest $100,000 into this seed round, and is guaranteed a bonus of 100% just by investing so early on. Billy is happy with this as he has an evil plan...

The second round, or the presale, is where most people get caught out. ICOs often promote attractive bonuses on a tight timeline to ensure urgency/scarcity. For example, if you invest this week you will get a 50% bonus but next week is only a 25% bonus etc.

Small investor Joe decides to invest $1,000 in the 50% bonus, pretty confident that he will be in profit.

The final round offers insignificant bonuses, maybe 10%. This is where the average punter Paul sticks a few hundred dollars in, not really caring about the outcome. They buy and hold for life.

Now the funding has ended and Billy, Joe and Paul are all waiting for their tokens.

Billy receives his tokens first, and also knows which exchanges the token is likely to be traded on first. Billy has his sell order at market ready, as he knows he will lock in a massive profit.

Joe is keeping a close eye on which exchange this token is likely going to be listed on, ready to act if needed.

Paul on the other hand, is down the pub telling everyone about this ICO that's about to make him a lot of money.

* The token is now tradable. *

Billy sells his entire holding, driving down the market but locking in over 50% ROI.

Joe manages to sell to break even, but is now very uncertain about the token's future.

Paul is down 50% but is confident that the "whales" are just accumulating more.

The only winners in this situation are the seed investors, who get the huge bonuses. I've seen this happen time and time again. For me, it is not worth the risk of investing in an ICO. Just wait until it hits the market and buy the initial dip.I've done this countless times and it works far better.

I'm sure there are great ICOs, and many people have made a significant amount by investing in them. But I understand how they are structured, and would rather not take that risk.

Secret 12: Dividends

Whilst dividends are commonly associated with the stock market, or with businesses in general. There is a selection of crypto assets which also pay dividends, but on a far more frequent basis.

To begin, let's define what a dividend is: a sum of money paid regularly (typically annually) by a company to its shareholders out of its profits (or reserves).

And let's change it for the crypto space: a sum of crypto tokens paid regularly (typically on a continual basis) by a company to its network participants out of its profits (or reserves or transaction fees, which is more common).

In the crypto space, there are two main ways you can earn dividends:

1) Staking – holding a token in a wallet
2) Holding – just holding a token in most wallets and even supporting exchanges

An emerging trend is for exchanges to have their own token, and to incentivise users to hold it by sharing a portion of the transaction fees. Other exchanges like Binance reduce your transaction fee by holding their token. It is seriously worth considering holding a portion of these exchange tokens, especially if you are going to be trading either very frequently or with a large amount.

Projects which have checked all the boxes of my due diligence and pay dividends are the potential unicorns for me. Of course, there are pros and cons to every investment, so let's go over those.

The Pros

Cryptos that pay dividends are still tradable on the wider market, meaning they have the same potential for capital appreciation as every other token out there. How is this a distinct pro? The advantage of buying dividend tokens is that, over time, whilst the price of the individual asset increases, so will your reward. Here's a quick example…

> *NEO pays a dividend token out called GAS, which trails NEO's price by around 50%. You buy enough NEO to get 1 GAS per week, which is around 350 NEO. At the time of purchasing, this cost you $5,000 (350 x 14.3). With GAS being roughly 50% of the price of NEO, you would be getting just over $7 per week. Which isn't a lot. BUT, if NEO hits $500 and GAS reaches $250, then you'd suddenly be getting $250 per week, or $1,000 per month. That's pretty good if you ask me, especially from an initial investment of only $5K.*

The second major advantage is that cryptos which pay dividends promote "holding" onto the token, rather than trading it. A lot of cryptos won't pay out your dividend unless you hold your token for a certain period of time. I would love to say that this decreases the volatility of these tokens, but that simply hasn't been true to date. Possibly, in the future, this could prevent such harsh downswings in price, which would then attract more investors to it, but the market seems too immature for that presently.

The Cons

While the promotion of holding can be seen as an advantage, the lock-up period that many tokens require can also be seen as a disadvantage. Whilst it is completely understandable that users are far more likely to trade the token if there are no "rules" in regards to the dividend payouts, requiring users to hold the token in a certain wallet for a long period of time also repels many investors from it. There are many cryptos which require you to hold their token for 30 days, or 60 consecutive days. There have been times where I've left a few days early and received nothing for holding it... a lot of people don't like being locked into a project, especially when the crypto markets are so choppy.

Another disadvantage of dividend tokens is that they are most probably going to be subject to income tax. At the time of writing this book, there are no clear parameters to what form of tax crypto dividends will be subject to, but I'm assuming it will be income tax (I hope I'm wrong). Obviously, the amount of tax you pay will be dependent on your income, but I know in the UK this figure can be as high as 45%. Ouch. Normal crypto gains are looking to be treated as capital gains tax, which is around 20% in the UK. So, the difference can be massive.

Masternoding is another alternative, where you stake some of your coins and then help verify the transactions on the network. By doing so you get a reward for it. I'm not an expert by any means when it comes to masternoding, so I tend to avoid it. The risks outweigh the rewards, in my opinion, and I know my strengths. If you are looking at doing masternoding, there are plenty of websites which show you how.

I focus on the easier, buy and hold type dividend tokens such as NEO and VET (make sure to do your own research if you are looking for dividend tokens – I may not be in these coins by the time you are reading this book. This market changes very fast).

To conclude this chapter, it's worth researching about these dividend tokens as the potential residual income can be vast. However, and this is really important, the vast majority are scams. Fraudsters promising weekly returns of extraordinary amounts just by investing in their token… just google "Bitconnect scam" and you'll see. I cannot emphasise how important it is to do your own research, even if you trust the source.

Secret 13: Mining

I'm sure you've heard about cryptocurrency mining, or how Bitcoin mining uses more electricity than the whole of New Zealand. If you currently mine, or are considering mining, I would urge you to read this chapter. Although I am against mining, I realise it can be profitable, dependent on which coin you mine etc. However, I'm going to be highlighting the reasons why I personally don't mine cryptos (and if you are a miner, it is worth considering these points).

First of all, the huge upfront costs. In order to have a reasonable size rig with the top end graphics cards and all the other components, you're looking at least £5,000. Once those costs are sunk, then you have to factor in the electricity costs for your mining rig. Unless you have free or subsidised electricity, you might never see a profit. Remember that most utility companies do not yet accept cryptocurrencies, so you'll need to liquidate your mined assets in order to pay for the bills. Which leads to the problem of then having to declare up to 45% income tax…

Best case scenario, your electricity is free/super cheap and you're profitably mining in a bullish trend. Worst case scenario, your electricity is expensive and you're running at a huge loss in a bearish market. What a lot of miners forget to mention is that their performance is directly correlated to the market trend.

"But my mining rig has value itself, which isn't corre-lated to the crypto market."

This is completely false. The cost of graphics cards soared in 2017 due to the demand for mining, meaning you are currently paying 5x more for the same graphics cards you could have got in 2016. If, for whatever reason (regulation, lack of profit etc.) miners stopped mining, guess what would happen... eBay would be flooded with graphics cards for sale and then the value of your mining rig would plummet (supply vs demand). The point I am trying to drive across is that the price of the mining rig is not as stable as miners say. I would factor this in if you are planning to mine.

Regulation... with the cost of electricity so high for mining, and the amount of electricity some of the larger tokens require, I would not be surprised if we started to see heavy regulation of mining companies. What happens if you're required to use renewable energy to power your mining rigs? What happens if your government imposes a tax on crypto mining operations (it really wouldn't surprise me)?

The ROI... I spoke with a leading mining expert in the UK, who shared the yearly performance of their mining rigs, and it was 1,000%. This number may seem massive, but it was actually worse than the market average. I know this is very dependent on what coins you mine, but then I could argue that investment ROI is dependent on what coin you invest in. I achieved over 3,000% ROI over the same period that mining achieved a 1,000% return. Yes, it does depend on many variables, but in my opinion, it's not worth it. Let's move on...

Secret 14: Event-Based Trading

We touched on this back when we spoke about hard forks, but very briefly. In a market where intrinsic value is very hard to measure (at the moment), investment decisions are almost entirely dependent on speculation. Speculation thrives off of events, which can be broken down as follows:

- Exchange listings (we've covered)
- Hard forks (we've covered)
- Rebranding
- Partnerships
- Events (conferences etc.)
- Development updates

Once I understood how to trade around all these "events", I significantly increased my ROI and reduced the massive drawdowns that I kept on having.

The fundamental rule is: Buy the rumour, sell the news.

This is quite a generic statement that is thrown around a lot in the crypto markets, but very few people actually know why this strategy is effective. I want to begin by stating that this strategy is not exclusive to the crypto market – the stock market behaves in a very similar fashion.

It really boils down to the media being a lagging indicator, and the public always getting in at the last minute

– it's human nature. Say, for example, there's one of the events above about to happen in 30 days' time. The price of that asset will likely increase leading up to the event, and then it will crash on the day of the event. This happens 90% of the time.

Here's why…

> Company X announces the event. Almost instantly, the active investors have acted on this announcement and have placed trades in this token. The price has likely increased a fair amount.

> Then, the wider market starts to pick up on this event, and the blogs and small news sites pick up on it too. This normally lasts a couple weeks before the bigger media sites decide to comment on this event.

> By this point, the price has increased a significant amount compared to a few weeks back and the event is right around the corner. Newer investors in the market are now both aware and excited about this event, while the investors who have been in this trade since the beginning are planning their exit. The event is further hyped by the token's community and team, drawing in more short-term speculators, who are all eager to buy the token on the day of the event.

> * The day of the event occurs. *

> Most investors who got in early on are now entirely out of this token, ready to buy the dip when it happens. The newer investor has just bought in, wait-

ing for the event and thinking about which Lambo he's going to buy after the event pushes the price to the moon.

* The event happens. *

And the price plummets. The smart investor's order fills at the low levels. But the newer investor is left confused, wondering why the price fell even though the event was good.

Here's why…

The market has already priced in the event.

This is so important I need to repeat it. If something is expected to happen, don't assume that the market will react when that event will happen. The market has likely already priced in that event and therefore, the expected outcome will not increase the price any further. People who are "in the know" about this sell to capitalise on profits and then the public panic-sells, and loses a significant amount of their investment. The market has already priced in the expected.

The next few chapters are going to go over all of these events, and give examples of how to trade them.

Secret 15: Rebranding

The market's reaction to projects rebranding is simply unbelievable, I'm sure many projects just rebrand for the sake of rebranding. This chapter will summarise what a rebranding is, how to profit from it, and a few examples of some crypto rebrands that have gone well.

So, what exactly do I mean by rebranding? Put simply, it's when a project decides to change their name, strategy and/or branding. It's a business pivot, after either realising a flaw in their current strategy or changing the vision of the project. In many cases, it makes sense to do so, especially in such a rapidly changing environment. One of the most common cases for rebranding is projects that were initially built on the Ethereum blockchain and then subsequently decide to shift onto their own. While I don't believe a name change in this situation is entirely necessary, it does add a "fresh" element to these projects. In their defence, they often add a few technical changes, such as dividends or changes to their block size/speed, which could be a potential reason for change.

The two most successful rebrands that I have seen are Antshares and Raiblocks. Just by reading these names, I'm sure you can see that they aren't the easiest to pronounce and sound a bit like kid's toys (lol). Anstshares is now known as NEO, and Raiblocks is now known as NANO.

Before Antshares changed to NEO, it was trading around $0.5. The hype around the change was not just the name, but the vision of the company, leading to a short-term increase to just under $50. NEO became labelled as the "Chinese Ethereum" and eventually peaked at $160 at the end of January 2018. Annoyingly, I found out about NEO after the rebrand, but I can see why investors got so excited about it. They introduced many new aspects to their project when it came to the rebranding, including dividends, a change in algorithm, becoming a blockchain angel investor and the NEO ecosystem. However, in my opinion, the largest change was the direct opposition to Ethereum, offering a solution for a far quicker and more robust ecosystem (potentially).

I have been in Raiblocks from the very early stages, and always questioned the name. It's hard to take it seriously… "Yeah, there's this project called Raiblocks and it looks super interesting" … right. The reason why I was in it so early on was due to the technology behind it – it's amazing. It allows for instant, almost fee-free transactions. Far more scalable than Bitcoin and uses nearly no computing power in comparison! Why aren't people speaking about Raiblocks? Well, the name is very off-putting. It's like the name Gertrude (no offence to anyone called Gertrude) – just by hearing it you might make an assumption about them. Same thing applies in the crypto space – with over 2,000 projects out there now, the name is very important. I think it was a very smart move for Raiblocks to change its name. Here's what they had to say… "The Core Team wanted a name that represented the simplicity and speed of the project, and Nano does just that."

Trading rebranding follows Secret 10: if you are aware of the rebranding, then the market has likely already priced it in. However, rebranding doesn't pop to the downside as much as other events. With the two examples above, they both increased in value after the rebranding was announced. This was mostly due to awareness, as they were both smaller projects which were suddenly brought into the limelight after their rebrand. I'd follow the rule of buying the rumour and selling the news, but perhaps only sell half, this time around. Worst case, you lose some profit from the 50% that remains in the market. Best case, it continues to increase and you gain on the 50% that's in, and then buy the token after a retracement.

Secret 16: Partnerships

Partnerships can often lead to the greatest short-term increase in price. However, partnerships are the most common for twisted truths and a very questionable form on delivering such announcements.

The term "partnership" is very vague, and perhaps unclear in the cryptocurrency space. For me, a partnership is where you are directly working with that company either by them providing your service, or they are using your blockchain to build their blockchain architecture. A "partnership" is not a website accepting payment in your crypto. Whilst this is great for adoption, this is hardly a partnership. I can accept Bitcoin as payment to EMIC – does that make me a partner of Bitcoin? The problem I have is the marketing associated with this form of partnership. A prime example of this is Verge's "partnership" with Pornhub (never heard of it ;-)). Verge raised a significant amount of their token in order to facilitate this "partnership". In other words... Verge paid Pornhub over $3 million USD just for them to accept XVG as a form of payment and call it a partnership. The hype around this mysterious announcement caused the price of Verge to increase over 100% during the month prior to the announcement. I remember warning the members of my club that owned Verge to sell the day before the event, and I'm glad I did as the price plummeted over 30% in just an hour, once the partnership was revealed.

Another great example of shady tokens using partnership hype is Tron. The founder of Tron, Justin Sun, tends to announce announcements. There's a funny meme* of the founder with the caption "Today I announce that tomorrow I will make an announcement." This type of marketing is just awful and lacks professionalism. Especially when all the founder seems to care about is the price of the asset. Hmm, maybe that's because he owns 5% of the entire supply personally.

You might be thinking that both those cases are obviously unprofessional and investors would steer clear of those projects. Ha! This is exactly what I thought, and I was entirely wrong. Projects like these actually increase the most. Yep, Verge increased by 1 million percent in 2017. Tron also increased by thousands of percent too. Why? Well, in a speculative market where the vast majority of investors can't be bothered to do even the most basic of due diligence and rely on announcements to make their investment decisions, the herd mentality kicks in and then the fear of missing out kicks in and all of a sudden, these projects are increasing by thousands of percent.

There is a lesson to be learnt from this. I used to get so annoyed at the immaturity of investors in this market, reacting to trivial announcements and spreading rumours just to pump the coin up in price. Until I learnt how to play them at their own game. I'm now announcing that in the next paragraph I'll be announcing how to do this.

Again, we come back to the foundational rule... Buy the rumour, sell the news. As soon as any project announces that they have an announcement or any hint of a partnership announcement in the near future, buy then, and sell before the event. Simple. This has made me a tremendous amount of money in the past, and works particularly well with "hype" coins like Tron and Verge.

Many people questioned why the price of Verge dropped by over 30% after their partnership with Pornhub. You probably have a good understanding as to why at this point... the market has already priced in the announcement.

* An image, video, piece of text, etc., typically humorous in nature, that is copied and spread rapidly by Internet users, often with slight variations.

Secret 17: Events

While "Events" is the umbrella term for all the secrets since Secret 14, this chapter is referring to physical crypto events and conferences. Out of all the "events", this has the smallest significance. However, there is one event that we need to cover.

Consensus. The largest cryptocurrency event hosted by CoinDesk, a cryptocurrency publisher. Over the course of the event, which was just three days long, the price of bitcoin went from $8,800 USD to $8,400 and then bounced back up for $8,800, to then fall over the next month down to the low $7K levels.

Why is this important? Just a few weeks prior to the event, bitcoin had tested the $10K levels again, and started to fall slowly as the event approached. The Twitter community and the vast majority of people in large Facebook groups were recommending to buy before the event as the price of bitcoin *has* always increased after consensus. Of course, it did not this year. In fact, it fell over 20% in the following weeks. **THE MARKET HAS ALREADY PRICED IN THE EXPECTED.** I firmly believe that early on in May, the larger capital started exiting the market in anticipation of this event, while the herd were buying in leading up to this event.

This expectation was such a buzz that there were even articles about bitcoin "mooning" after this event, which of course turned out to be false. I don't trade events, as they are much more difficult to trade and rely on sentiment more than anything. As we were in a bearish trend in 2018, the probabilities were that the price would keep on falling, regardless of the event. But for some reason, the majority of the market seemed to think otherwise. Just a month after the event, bitcoin was down over 30%. This would have been heavily due to the loss of faith many investors had. Historic trends are indicators, but they are not set in stone. One lesson I've learnt is to test every strategy/indicator myself during live market conditions and then make conclusions. This is probably why I've lost a lot of money in the past, but it's how I've learnt what works, and what does not. While I'm trying to keep this book evergreen, as the market matures, some of these "secrets" will either not work at all, or have a much smaller effect. I will be continuously testing, and so should you.

This secret was really just to share that events don't actually correlate that much to the market direction. Sure, there was some volatility in the market during this year's Consensus conference. However, this did not stop the market falling. Don't fall into the "hype" trap – you will almost definitely lose money.

Secret 18: Development Updates

Development updates are very unique to the cryptocurrency space, while still following the foundational rule of "Buy the rumour, sell the news." Development updates require a little digging to forecast "when" they will be completed.

The main types of development updates you need to look out for are:

- Hard forks (we've covered this)
- Testnet launch
- Mainnet launch
- Anything else (if it sounds technical, people still tend to buy)

To begin this chapter, let's define what a testnet and a mainnet are.

Bitcoin Wiki defines Testnet as: The testnet is an alternative Bitcoin blockchain, to be used for testing. Testnet coins are separate and distinct from actual bitcoins, and are never supposed to have any value. This allows application developers or bitcoin testers to experiment, without having to use real bitcoins or worrying about breaking the main bitcoin chain.

My definition: A testnet is where the developers can play around with the code, without affecting the value of the token on the mainnet. Most projects create their testnet before moving onto their very own mainnet.

Bitcoin Wiki defines Mainnet as: The main network wherein actual transactions take place on a distributed ledger; this is in contrast to the testnet, or test network, where new Dapps and EDCCs can be tested and developed.

My definition: Pretty much the same as the above. Mainnet is where the live transactions occur (transaction meaning anything from data to the tokens themselves).

One last definition… tokens. A cryptocurrency "token" is a cryptocurrency that has been built on another network. For example, most projects out there were built on the Ethereum network, and they are referred to as ERC-20 tokens.

If they are built on their own network, they are referred to as "coins" or crypto "assets". Very confusing terminology, I know. But for now, we just need to understand that some cryptos are built on their own network, while others are built on an existing network (tokens).

One of the shifts I have been noticing in 2018 is the change from "tokens" to independent coins. Put simply, crypto projects have been building their own network, instead of building on top of another. A few examples of well-known projects that have done this are EOS, Tron and Vechain. There are two main reasons for the shift. The first major reason is mostly to address the scalability issues that some of the origin networks face. The second reason is that the plan for that project all along was to create their own independent blockchain, but used the origin platform for crowdfunding.

I fully expect this trend to continue going forward, and oddly enough, you can profit from it too.

With all development updates, the first place to look would be the roadmap of that project. This will be located either in their whitepaper or on their associated website. Most roadmaps have clear development deadlines (normally stated in quarters). Knowing roughly when a significant development update should be due can put you miles in front of the herd. Yes, it does require some research, but most people won't do this research at all, and will wait until the announcement comes through to then buy that asset. That is when you will be selling.

Back to "testnet" and "mainnet". For some odd reason, most of the time a project goes through this process of moving onto their own network, the price will increase, normally starting from the testnet and then leading up until the mainnet. So, understanding the expected dates can help you plan your trading of that asset.

Side note: Make sure you follow the projects which are moving onto their own network. The current "tokens" will no longer be valid on their new network, so you'll need to convert your tokens to ensure you don't lose them. Binance tends to do this for you, and most of the time I'll stick my tokens there for ease.

I appreciate that this chapter can be very confusing, with all the technical jargon. To summarise in simple terms, now that you are aware of these events, and where to find them, you can plan your trades of these assets in advance, based on this knowledge you have.

Twitter is also a good place to follow most projects. For some reason, most announcements happen on there, so it's worth following the CEOs/lead developers of each project, and each project's official Twitter account.

Secret 19: The Media

Where to start… Information is your best friend, yet your worst enemy. The sources you choose will greatly determine your investment return. Most publications are privately owned by corporations with **their** best interests in mind, not yours. This chapter will be covering how the media is manipulated, how to find trustworthy sources, and how nuggets of information can help you make a great profit in this market.

CNBC have a reputation for being a contrarian indicator. When Ripple was trading at its all-time high, they did a CNBC special, showing investors how to BUY Ripple. When Ripple hit its 2018 low, they then did a special, showing investors how to SELL Ripple. That's right, buy high, sell low.

If you follow the routes, you'll find that CNBC is owned by Comcast, who are the world's biggest entertainment company. Comcast is a publicly listed company, with the biggest shareholders being The Vanguard Group and Blackrock. The reason why I am mentioning this is to point out that all of these media giants have shareholders to answer to. Quite often they will present "news" that will get attention (as that brings revenue), not necessarily what is true.

It amazes me how often I see the same articles posted time and time again during certain market conditions.

Every single dip this year I've seen CNBC share articles about "the Bitcoin bubble bursting" or some form of fear. Why do they do this?

Well, there are two reasons…

1) **Attention.** During times of fear in the market, investors are looking to rationalise the reasoning behind the fall. Often, there is no reason, and it's just the market moving. Yet CNBC will ALWAYS have a reason for the fall.

2) **Manipulation.** The trading community and those "in the know" often preach about how the media is manipulated, and I agree. However, it is very hard to find proof of this, as it would almost certainly be illegal. Here is what the "whales" * do…

Say you had multimillions or even billions under management, and wanted to get into the cryptocurrency market. You are not going to be buying anywhere near the highs. With such a large amount of capital, you have the power to drive down prices massively (we'll speak about this in greater detail in the next chapter). To ensure the price moves down, what stops you paying a few journalists to spread some negative news in the market, while you short it on the futures market and sell any holdings you have? Well, nothing. Especially in such an unregulated market, and with such a small market cap. This is exactly what happens in the background. The large players use the media to ensure that the market moves in the direction as intended. Why do they need the public to sell? Liquidity.

In order for a seven, eight or nine-figure buy order to be filled, there needs to be sufficient volume at that price level (we discussed slippage and volume in Secret 6). So, the whales get the public to sell at the level they want to buy at. So, when CNBC was telling everyone to sell at all-time lows, who do you think was buying those sell orders?

So, you may be questioning where to find reputable sources, and this is where the difficulty is. There are a few definitions that I need to highlight before I share some sources that I use...

Shill: This is someone who promotes one coin heavily. The behaviour of some people is cultish. Many even change their Twitter handles to include the coin that they are shilling.

Make sure to follow me on Twitter: @XRP_Dev (that's a joke by the way... my actual Twitter is @devinmilsom).

P&D: Pump and dump groups are a) illegal and b) very immoral. I'll dive into the details in a later chapter, but it is important to reference now – and most P&D groups are filled with shills.

I often find that those who "shill" certain coins often have some great information about that coin. Obviously that information is only positive, but it is worth starting with this, as they've often done some deep digging to find every reason to support that coin as possible.

Once you have a good understanding of the project, and all the benefits of it, I would simply google the coin's name and then "scam" at the end. You're bound to find tonnes of articles/videos highlighting all the negatives of the project.

Now you have a balanced view of all the pros and cons of this project, and can make a reasonable judgement as to whether or not you should invest in the project. However, it is important to consider all the secrets that have been shared before investing in any project.

Below is a list of sources I use for information.

Articles

www.cryptoinvestorsblog.com – This is my blog.

www.cointelegraph.com – A leading crypto news site.

https://medium.com/@devinmilsom – Great selection of articles from a wide selection of writers. This is the URL to my profile.

https://www.quora.com/profile/Devin-Milsom-1 – Quora is a great place to get any questions answered by some very knowledgeable people. Be VERY careful of self-proclaimed "experts." I was the No.1 Writer for both cryptocurrencies and Bitcoin throughout 2017, and have over 2 million answer views. I have learnt a tremendous amount about other Quora writers whilst I was very active on the platform, and had many "experts" message me personally trying to get people in pump and dump groups etc.... Word of advice: avoid anyone who claims to be an "expert".

Videos

YouTube channels that I follow:

Devin Milsom – My own. I don't follow it (lol) but thought I'd share.

Crypto Daily – The funniest crypto YouTuber out there, and very informative too.

Boxmining – One of the best analysts out there.

Others worth mentioning: **Ivan on Tech, Datadash** and **Doug Polk Crypto.**

Of course, this is just my opinion. I wouldn't follow too many cryptocurrency influencers, as you will get very conflicting opinions. I've just picked a few that I use as a secondary form of research.

The last section I want to mention about the news/media is how valuable information can be. The market prices itself based on known information, as mentioned previously. However, it is in the depths where you can find golden nuggets of information that can lead to you having information before the majority of the market. As mentioned before, following all the projects and their team on Twitter, joining the telegram groups and actively reading Reddit posts can be very rewarding. It is often in these places (and some of the sources listed above) where you can find leaks and rumours that can help you decide on a positioning in or out of a crypto. What often happens is a small minority of the wider community will find out about some key information, and this is often shared on social networks. Then the bloggers pick up on it, and share it to their communities and then the big boys pick up on it, but normally last. If you are seeing information on CNBC, it is likely that the market priced this information in days ago.

I want to conclude this chapter by referring back to the beginning chapters of this book. Controlling your emotions to make logical decisions will determine whether you make a profit or fall, from the fear of missing out. It is easy to see a bullish article and go and buy that coin, but it takes emotional discipline to realise that the market has already priced in this news, and actually, there may be a high probability of the coin falling in price. Whenever you feel FOMO, just take a step back, examine the facts and then proceed. If you want a second opinion, just send me an email. Opportunities come by very frequently – I've let hundreds go before. Yes, it stings a small amount when you see a coin you were going to get into increase a significant amount while you sat on the sidelines. BUT, I've seen coins crash massively, and I've been glad I didn't pull the trigger on those occasions.

I'd rather be out of an investment wishing I was in, than in an investment wishing I was out... remember, there's another opportunity right around the corner.

* A whale is a person or corporation that has a lot of capital (multimillions – billions).

Secret 20: Pump and Dump Schemes

I've had multiple emails asking me where to find the best pump and dump schemes… I'm not sure whether or not they realise it, but P&D schemes are illegal. It is fraud. Let me explain how P&D schemes work. I'll pretend to be the villain…

> So, I've just created a group and attracted 1,000 members in it. I've called this group "Pump Master Whales (lol)". I've told everyone that the announcement will be at 7:00PM and the exchange they need to be on is Binance.
>
> I then log in to Binance at 6:00PM and find a coin with a very low volume, but enough to get my order filled – let's call this "Devcoin".
>
> I buy as much of Devcoin as I can before 6:55PM.
>
> I then broadcast to the group that "Devcoin" is about to moon and that they need to buy as much as possible. To make it look official, I tell them to sell at a level way above where I will be selling.
>
> The group pumps the price, I sell, I make a lot of profit from this, and maybe a select few others in the group do too (the ones that got in first).

Those select few then leave testimonials, which I use to promote the group further.

I know that the majority of members in the group will lose money, but I also know that I will always make money and always have a select few that make some money… so I can use them to market the P&D group going forward.

I despise P&D groups. They give crypto a bad name. As mentioned before, it is illegal and very immoral. Every person who invites me to a P&D group, I have and will continue to publicly expose.

But it gets a little more complicated…

Of course, P&D scammers have realised that most semi-informed investors can realise pump and dump schemes are a scam. So, what do they do? They call themselves "signal" groups. There are hundreds of these, and many, many people fall for them. Unfortunately, there is no easy way of spotting which are legitimate, and which are P&D schemes. The key difference is that signal groups tend to be membership-based, whereas most P&D groups are free.

Key takeaway: Avoid P&D groups, or any free "signal" groups. You will more than likely lose a lot of capital.

Secret 21: Trading Bots

I have spent thousands of pounds on various trading bots (just to test) and absolutely none of them have worked. 99% of bots out there are a load of rubbish, and the only reason they sell is because the marketing is excellent.

Don't waste your time and money with trading bots.

I could end the chapter here, but there are a few further points I want to highlight about trading bots.

The definition of a trading bot in this sense is a "magic" strategy that makes guaranteed profits no matter what market condition. Sounds good, right?

Everyone is searching for that one golden strategy that will make money for them while they sleep. This does not exist. Unfortunately, human nature is attracted to get rich quick schemes, and bots are the king of them all. There are a few crypto bots who it is claimed were created by a "legendary" trader. Guess what? After doing some research, I inevitably find that this person **does not exist.** Do not believe anything you read of these websites. Normally a good Google search of the trading bot's name + scam will reveal the truth behind these bots.

The main reason why I purchased many bots was to see what was out there. I was going to create my own bot for EMIC based on some of the really successful indicators that I had been using. After many hours of back-testing and research, I realised that it was simply not profitable. It was an expensive lesson to learn, and I could have very easily released a bot that has some historic profitability, but in such a rapidly changing market, it wouldn't last very long at all. I value my reputation far more than quick, immoral money.

When should you use a bot?

There is one type of bot that I am not against, and that is a trailing stop loss bot. All this bot does is place a trailing exit signal to get you out of a trade. Say for example you are in a crypto and it shoots up 50%, your trailing stop will follow it as it continues to climb, and then the moment it falls to a certain level, it will sell and lock your profit in. Stop losses can also be used as an insurance if you are wrong. Say you think a coin will shoot up, so you go buy/go long. After a few days, the price drops – however, this will trigger your stop and get you out sooner, rather than having to accept the loss/hold.

One of the fundamental rules of trading/investing is: Cut your losses short, and let your profits run.

Key takeaway: Trading bots can be very useful tools for mitigating risk, but I would never trust any "secret" strategies that many bots promise.

[BONUS] Secret 22: "Experts" and Other Scams

I firmly believe that having a mentor or someone with great knowledge in a market can be very beneficial, from both an investment perspective and by gaining valuable knowledge. When I first started investing, I followed a few expert traders, and learnt a tremendous amount from them. One of them helped me massively, and I am glad that I paid for his service when I was first starting. But the other one charged an excessive amount for regurgitated information that he did not fully understand himself, giving trades which had every possible outcome under the sun and then blaming the students when they lost money.

You will never hear me calling myself an expert – I am not. I have been investing for around three years and in the crypto market for around two years. I have a good understanding of the technology behind many of these cryptos, and a good understanding of investing/trading. However, I also have a very good understanding of marketing, and every tactic many businesses use to lure customers in.

I'm not going to name call, but I will highlight the tactics that many fake "experts" use to trick the average investor into buying their course or subscribing to their newsletters etc.

Most of the marketing stems back to the psychology of humans. Everyone wants to get rich quick. So, what do these marketers do? They play on this emotion big time. They'll claim that they know which coin will increase by thousands of percent, and the only way to know is by buying their newsletters. They will also spam you with ads and (fake) testimonials from their subscribers making thousands of percent ROI.

Why do they do it? Because it works. They will be making millions from selling the shovels during the gold rush. However, they aren't selling shovels at all. They are selling plastic spoons.

Here are a few rules that I use when I consider advisors in a sector...

What is their personal return in the market (to date)? A lot of these marketers do not share such information, as it leaves them vulnerable to the truth!

What is their free content like? I look for valuable articles, videos, reports to establish whether or not they know what they are talking about.

Testimonials... Real people, and real testimonials. Ignore very generic testimonials as these are easily faked. I ask my members to leave testimonials on my Facebook page as this can't be faked. Try looking on Facebook first.

Are they promising returns? This is an immediate red flag. There are no guarantees in any market. This annoys me the most, because I see uninformed investors falling for this all the time.

Do they give every option under the sun? This shows a lack of competence. You often see videos that are very long and seem "technical" but essentially say "the price might go up, down or sideways"... that's helpful! I understand that investing is all about probabilities and risk mitigation, but even still, you should give one clear signal and accept that you will be wrong sometimes and clearly explain this.

Can you contact them personally? A lot of the fraudulent "experts" will stay as far away from customer communication as possible. If you are going to be trusting someone, surely you should be able to at least email them (and get a response)?

And then finally, my gut feeling. Is this person trying to help me, or trying to just take my money?

Here are a few other common scams...

Earn Bitcoin Daily – Scammers love this one. They promise daily returns and lure people in. This is either a Ponzi scheme or they'll just take your funds and you won't hear from them again.

Earn FREE Bitcoin – Again, no such thing. It's like me saying "earn free dollars"... you'd tell me to ~~fuck off~~ go away.

Physical Bitcoin – Please do not fall for this. This actually happened a lot in the 2017 December rally. I've actually bought a few hundred physical bitcoins, as they look cool. But they have no connection in price to the digital asset called bitcoin. Many scammers were selling these physical coins (which you can get for £1) for the market price of BTC.

Send 1 BTC and Get 5 BACK – Twitter has really cracked down on this. But I still see this everywhere. There is no such thing. Scammers will impersonate a CEO or company and pretend to be giving away a huge amount of ETH or BTC, and all you have to do is send 1 BTC to them and they'll send 10 back! They then set bots to reply, saying, "OMG can't believe this worked, thought it was a scam but I've got 10 BTC in my address, thanks *CEO/company name*" to fool people further. I can't even guess how much this scam has taken from people, but it will be in the eight or nine-figure range.

Be careful of links – There are so many copycat websites that are created to steal your login details. Make sure to triple check every URL!

www.bīnance.com – did you notice the accent on the "I"? That takes you to an entirely different place. Be very careful.

Never click on suspicious links in emails, be very careful downloading suspicious files and make sure to have Internet security running at all times.

I want to conclude this chapter by pointing out that there are genuine, honest people in this market that you can trust, and they can help you greatly. I hope that I am one of these people to you. It's just a shame that there are also some very greedy immoral people that don't care about you at all, they just want your money. I suppose that is life, the good and the bad, the yin and the yang.

[BONUS] Secret 23: Selling

The final secret I want to share with you is that you need to sell at some point. Now, this may seem like common sense, but unfortunately the mentality of the market is to just hold on for dear life (HODL). If you never realise profits, then what is the point in investing? Market spectators watch the price of their assets go to all-time highs, and then watch them fall all the way back down. This is why the vast majority eventually lose money in bubbles. I have spoken to many paper millionaires in this space who have watched their portfolio fall by more than 90% and still remained blindly bullish.

I remember everyone speaking about what Lamborghini they were going to buy in December, after making significant profits. Instead of averaging out, or taking their initial investment out, they just held and hoped for the market to continue rising. We all know how this turned out.

Greed is a very powerful emotion, it causes severe confirmation bias and leads to herd mentality, which always loses over a longer period of time. Fear is the superior emotion. As the famous saying goes: "The bull climbs the stairs and the bear jumps out the window." Your portfolio will be slaughtered during a downtrend. Remember, if you lose 50% of your portfolio, you don't need a 50% increase to break even, you need a 100% return.

So, you're probably questioning when exactly to sell. I wish this was a simple answer. The short answer is that no-one knows exactly when the top or bottom of any market is. However, there are a few exit signals that I use, and will be using going forward.

Sentiment

The widespread sentiment is a very good indicator. When everybody is extremely bullish, you should consider averaging out. When everyone is extremely bearish, you should consider averaging in.

Warren Buffet once said, "Be fearful when others are greedy and greedy when others are fearful." This applies in every market, as they are all driven by human emotions.

When your taxi driver, hairdresser and the general public start advising you which crypto assets to buy, it's time to sell. Joe Kennedy publicly stated, "You know it's time to sell when shoeshine boys give you stock tips. This bull market is over." He said this right before the great depression, and by taking the contrarian view, it made him a very wealthy man.

Market Cap

This number is far harder to predict. Some "experts" think it will go to 20 trillion, others think the "bubble" has already burst. My personal prediction is that the market cap will reach near 10 trillion before bursting. 99% of the crypto projects will then crash and never recover, and the remaining 1% will be the blue-chip cryptos that go onto performing like the FANG stocks. Could it go higher? Of course; markets tend to trend a lot longer than anyone can ever expect. I'm just going to start averaging out near this level.

Market cap is a secondary; sentiment is far more important. The market cap is driven by demand, which is driven by greed and fear. This is why sentiment is the best indicator when jumping in/out of a market.

Once you have doubled your investment, take your original capital out. This is something I did to reduce the stress about losing money, after making a large amount of profit, I took out my original investment and was left with profit to play with. This massively reduces the emotional attachment you have with the market, which will help you make far more rational decisions.

Average Out!

Your trades and investments do not need to be all or nothing. People feel like they often have to entirely enter or exit the market. This is not true, and will sting you when you are wrong. I learnt this lesson the hard way...

I bought a crypto called Cardano (ADA) right at its inception at $0.02. Over the next few months, it increased a significant amount to $0.1 – over 500% ROI. In one day, it went from $0.05 to $0.1 – a 100% increase! I thought that I knew it would retrace, so I sold my entire Cardano holdings, and then... it kept on rising to $0.15. I then let my emotions take control and jumped back in at that level and it dropped to $0.12! Painful, expensive lesson.

Just remember, you don't have to exit or enter any trade 100%. You can always average in, and average out.

The Six Successes

Before I shared the secrets, I shared some of the painful lessons I learnt when I first started investing in this market. I am glad that these events happened. Without them I would have never been able to grow my portfolio as much as I did, and I would've never been able to write this book.

As we get towards the end of the book, I want to share some of the more successful investments I have made and hope that they inspire you, whether you are a first-time investor or have been in the market a while and been through some rough rides!

#001 Cardano

Cardano is one of the best investments I've made, and one that I am super proud of too. I spent days researching Cardano. I read through their whitepaper, which was very technical and I really struggled to understand it at the time, but I was keen to understand more. I then watched several videos of the founder, Charles Hoskinson, speaking with such passion about the vision for Cardano. He spoke about it in very simple terms, making it understandable to anyone. I later found out that he was an early contributor to Ethereum, the second largest crypto asset at the time and I put a significant amount of capital towards the project as soon as it hit the market – at $0.02. Cardano peaked at $1.15, a 5,750% increase in

3 months. Pretty good, right? I didn't exit right at the top, I exited around half my holdings from $0.5–$1.1, which was still pretty good. Money aside, there is no better feeling than when you put in the time and effort to research something, and then see your efforts paying off.

#002 NEO

NEO was another great investment of mine; I got in this one just before I got into Cardano. NEO was labelled as the "Chinese Ethereum" so it got my attention pretty quickly. As with all my investments, I spend a long time studying it. I found many very interesting facts that drew me into investing in NEO. One of the main reasons was that the founder has a good relationship with the Chinese government and not only helped advise them about blockchain technology, but actually assisted them with their regulation. NEO was also my first crypto that paid dividends, which was cool (and profitable).

I got into NEO around $10, and it peaked around $160 (1,600% ROI), which was great. What I loved more (and still do) is the value of the dividend token – GAS – which trails the price of NEO around 50%. I was getting a fair amount of this token for just holding NEO! I just sold my GAS and used it to buy other cryptos, which was a win-win for me!

#003 Verge

Towards the end of December, I had learnt a few vital lessons. Verge had a huge announcement at the end of the year, a way of changing between completely private transactions and traceable transactions. This was a great concept, and I knew the community would be very excited about this.

I bought Verge as soon as the announcement was released, a couple weeks before it was due to take place, and experienced a nice 2000% increase in price leading up to the event (a lot of this was due to the December rally).

Knowing that the price dumps most of the time when announcements are made, I sold the day before the event and witnessed it plummet 40% after the event was delayed by just five minutes and then released, which overwhelmingly seemed a disappointment!

I then sold the majority of my profits from Tron…

#004 Tron

This trade made me over £50,000. I had just sold Verge for Tron, after doing some further research, knowing they had some announcement in a couple weeks and the fact that it was a relatively unknown crypto at the time. In one week, I made around £50,000.

#005 Selling in January

This was luck combined with the knowledge that the prices of cryptos were very overbought. My portfolio had just reached an all-time high, and I decided to take some profits off the table. I took around half out at the time (wish I'd taken it all out – lol) and used a lot of it as celebration capital…

This year I've been to Rome with my girlfriend, and was fascinated with the beauty of the architecture. I've been to the Caribbean with my family where I went scuba diving for the first time. I remember, on our second dive, we got circled by a six-foot reef shark!

I've also booked an entire month in the USA early 2019, to go to several business/investing events to see some of my role models speak and to learn from them. Oh, and we're going to Disney World/Universal too for a couple weeks (never too old to go there!).

If I hadn't invested in this market, I would have never been able to experience these amazing events.

#006 Getting out at $11.7K

I've made many good short trades this year (2018), but my best was from $11.7K down to the $8K levels. Exiting the market at these levels saved me a lot of capital and allowed me to double my holdings without having to add more capital to the market, which was awesome.

I wrote a blog post on this and a few Quora posts about this trade the day before it happened. Just look there if you want proof.

Final Words

I hope you have found the information in this book extremely valuable, and I hope you make a significant profit by learning from my mistakes. The reason why I wrote this book was to share the lessons I had learnt in the crypto market and hope that you don't make the same mistakes that I did.

I am extremely passionate about investing and business; they truly are the best vehicles to accumulate wealth in a relatively short period of time. I was able to quit my job, travel across the world and start a business around what I love doing because of my investments in an asset class that many would tell you to avoid. If you currently have any of these goals, I hope I am an inspiration as to what is possible. Opportunities are everywhere – when you start looking.

I wish you all the best,

Devin Milsom

Feel free to contact me here:
devin@emergingmarketsinvestmentclub.com
(I love to hear success stories, so please share!)

What's Next?

1) (If you are already in the market, skip to step 2) ...

   If you have risk capital to invest, then I would look into cryptocurrencies as an asset class and structure an investment allocation to it. That could be as little as 1% or as much as you are willing to risk. Remember you can always average into the market; it's what I do.

2) Join **Emerging Markets Investment Club.**

--> www.emergingmarketsinvestmentclub.com/book **<--**

Emerging Markets focuses on emerging markets, and cryptocurrencies are certainly one of them! EMIC is beneficial for people who:

1. Are just getting started
2. Have little time to follow the market
3. Don't know how to trade
4. Have or plan on investing more than $1,000 in the market

I remember how difficult it was for me to keep up with this wild market after a long day at work. I would get home at 6PM and then spend from 7PM–12AM studying, trading and blogging. It was exhausting, and wouldn't be possible if I had kids or other commitments. When I first got started, everything was so confusing: wallets, private keys, knowing what to invest in and so on. I also remember being annoyed seeing my portfolio increase significantly, just to halve during a dip. I'm sure you've had similar experiences before.

This was the main reason why I created Emerging Markets Investment Club, to help you invest and trade in this market, without taking too much time out of your life.

Here's what you'll get:

Access to My Trades: This alone is very valuable, you can choose to follow exactly what I do, LIVE. I put my money where my mouth is, and I am open and transparent with my trades.

Access to EMIC's Training Portal: Consisting of over 10 hours of extremely valuable content, ranging from the absolute basics of the crypto space to advanced trading techniques. Part of the membership also includes lifetime upgrades to all courses that are on the membership portal.

Access to My Private Facebook Community: This is where the community asks questions, shares articles and congregates. It's an amazing place and I learn a tremendous amount every day from the content that is shared.

Cryptotools.co.uk: After having to have 16 tabs open to access various websites that help me invest in the market, I decided to create my own "tool" website and put them all in one place. This website will eventually have hundreds of tools that will help save and make you money in the space. Only members of EMIC have access to this website.

"Blackbox": I like to keep this one a secret. You'll have to join to find out. ;-)

The reason why I mention having at least $1,000 invested in the market is that I know that from this level and above is where I can deliver an extreme amount of value in comparison to the membership fee. If you only have a couple hundred dollars, I have a few resources for you that I will mention at the end of the book. My personal goal is to provide at least 10x in value than you'll ever pay for the club.

Here's the link to join again:

--> www.emergingmarketsinvestmentclub.com/book <--

P.S. As an added bonus, you'll receive a complimentary portfolio review, where I personally look through your portfolio and provide comments based on my experience – but this is not financial advice.

Free Resources

If you are just starting out, here's a free training portal that will get you on your feet:

www.emergingmarketsinvestmentclub.com/freetraining

www.cryptoinvestorsblog.com – My blog.

Where to find me:

@DevinMilsom – my Twitter and Quora.

Devin Milsom – Facebook, YouTube and pretty much everything else.

Again, I hope you've enjoyed this book. I would be very grateful if you could leave feedback on Amazon or Facebook.

All the best,

Devin Milsom

31291230R00078

Printed in Poland
by Amazon Fulfillment
Poland Sp. z o.o., Wrocław